I
AM
ZION

JOHN ECKHARDT

CHARISMA
HOUSE

Copyright © 2020 by John Eckhardt
All rights reserved

Visit the author's website at www.johneckhardt.global.

Library of Congress Cataloging-in-Publication Data
Names: Eckhardt, John, 1957- author.
Title: I am Zion / by John Eckhardt.
Description: Lake Mary, Florida : Charisma House, [2019] | Includes bibliographical references.
Identifiers: LCCN 2019020867 (print) | LCCN 2019981461 (ebook) | ISBN 9781629996219 (trade paperback) | ISBN 9781629996226 (ebook) Subjects: LCSH: Spiritual life--Christianity. | Christian life.
Classification: LCC BV4501.3 .E325 2019 (print) | LCC BV4501.3 (ebook) | DDC 248.4--dc23
LC record available at https://lccn.loc.gov/2019020867
LC ebook record available at https://lccn.loc.gov/2019981461

20 21 22 23 24 — 987654321
Printed in the United States of America

CONTENTS

Introduction

A CHOSEN PLACE
FOR A CHOSEN PEOPLE

For the LORD hath chosen Zion; he hath desired it for his
habitation. This is my rest for ever: here will I dwell; for I
have desired it. I will abundantly bless her provision: I will
satisfy her poor with bread. I will also clothe her priests
with salvation: and her saints shall shout aloud for joy.
—PSALM 132:13–16

ZION IS ONE of the most important topics in Scripture, yet we
do not teach much about it. The revelation concerning Zion
has been all but lost in today's church. It is one of my favorite subjects because I believe the spiritual significance of Zion is one of
the most important revelations you can have as a child of God.
Locked up within the mysteries of Zion are the eternal plans and
purposes of God for all His children.

Studying God's plans and purposes gives us insight into His
wisdom. And when you access the realm of God's wisdom, special
blessings are always the result. The Bible says throughout Proverbs
that wisdom brings riches (3:16; 8:18), favor (3:4; 8:35), and promotion (4:8).

I have learned that the more I understand and walk in the plans
and purposes of God, the more wisdom comes into my life. And
the more that wisdom comes into my life, the more I experience
the blessing of God. God imparts wisdom when we seek to understand and yield to His plans, purposes, and will.

In the Old Testament—the age of the prophets, priests, and

kings—and even into the New Testament with the apostles, the plan of God was a mystery. The apostle Paul wrote about the mysteries of God throughout his epistles as God gave him. These revealed mysteries revolved around the church, or the body of Christ (Heb. 12:22–23); the kingdom (Mark 4:11), which is established in Zion; and the revelation of Christ Himself (Col. 1:27; 2:2–3). These were hidden things. They were mysteries. They were the hidden wisdom of God, which God revealed to Paul apostolically; Paul then revealed them to the saints through his teachings and writings, even while in chains.

One thing we need to understand concerning Zion and the apostolic anointing is that the purpose of the apostolic anointing is to bring insight, revelation, and understanding to God's people concerning His plans, purposes, and will. The function of the apostolic is to unlock the mysteries of the kingdom of God so that people can begin to gain understanding and embrace the plan and purpose of God for their lives. If it had not been for Paul's function under the weight of his apostolic call and anointing, we would not be able to search the Scriptures for this present truth of the reality of Zion. I will talk more about Zion and the apostolic in later chapters.

What we need to know now, however, is that the enemy worked overtime to keep these revelations from being released so we could not walk in the benefits of them. Paul suffered great persecution as he went from church to church and city to city, preaching the revelations of Christ, the kingdom, heavenly Zion, and the full measure of the gospel. Yet these are the very revelations we must have knowledge of to take hold of the abundant life in Christ.

Christ is the cornerstone of Zion (1 Pet. 2:6). The revelation of Christ unlocks the mystery of Zion, which holds the plan of God for you and me. When we get an understanding and a revelation of the plans and purposes—the mysteries—of God, we increase in God's wisdom, and when you increase in God's wisdom, get ready for promotion.

We will discover that the revelation of Zion is a revelation of the glory of God. And in the glory of God it is impossible to stay small, insignificant, unnoticed, or forgotten. You can do nothing but increase in every area when the glory invades your life, because God does not do small when it comes to His glory.

THE KEY TO PROMOTION AND INCREASE

People often ask me, "What is the key to success?" "What is the key to promotion?" I always tell them, "Wisdom is the principal thing." When you get wisdom, understanding, revelation, and insight into the plans and purposes of God, get ready for breakthrough. Get ready for prosperity. Get ready for abundance. Get ready for promotion. But you will not get insight and wisdom in a church where all they do is whoop and holler. You need teaching, instruction, insight, revelation, and understanding of the wisdom of God that brings the apostolic into play. Part of the apostolic ministry is to establish order and foundation in the body of Christ. This is what Paul was establishing in the first-century church at great peril and risk to his physical body. He suffered much persecution bringing revelation to the people of God concerning God's ultimate plan for them beyond the plan of salvation. The revelation of Zion goes beyond just being saved. When you understand who you are in relationship to Zion, everything changes.

There is a key to exaltation, promotion, and all the good things God has for us through understanding this biblical mystery of Zion. If you attend a church, you need to make sure it is a Zion church, and you will need to know what you are looking for to recognize those qualifying characteristics. You need to be among a people who know how to tap into the glory of Zion in worship. We will discuss why this is so important throughout the book, but the first thing to know is that Zion represents the place God has chosen as His dwelling place. Therefore Zion churches are the places God has chosen to dwell. If it is not a Zion church, God's presence doesn't manifest there. We make a lot of choices in our lives, including what church we go to, based on what we want and not based on what God wants—what He chooses. But as we come into this revelation of Zion, we should understand how important it is to choose what God chooses. If God chooses Zion, we should too.

As I will explain, Zion is more than a physical place; it is now a state of spiritual being. When we live with this understanding, life as we know it goes to a whole other level. If you want to enjoy God's best, you need to be in the best place, and the best place needs to reside in you. This is a place called Zion. In this book I will help you know what Zion is, how to identify it, how to know when you've arrived, and what happens when you are not in Zion.

As a Zion believer, when it comes to being part of an assembly or church, or making decisions in life altogether, the priority is not your preferences. What matters is God's choice, and He chooses Zion. So many people make decisions based on certain characteristics they find appealing—qualities that have nothing to do with Zion. But I want to show how having a Zion heart calls you out of feeding the desire of a heart bound to limitations and restrictions of the world. Sin and carnality limit us. The enemy has fooled man into believing the lie that any good can come from rejecting what God chooses, and that is never the case. We must develop a heart that desires what God desires. God desires Zion.

COME OUT OF BABYLON AND INTO ZION

In my book *The Good Land* I discussed how the people of Israel could not crossover into the Promised Land until they shed their Egypt and wilderness mentality. A whole generation had to die off before they could enter the land. But even as they dwelled in the good land, the people rebelled against God. They disobeyed Him over and over again until He led them back into captivity—this time by the hands of the Babylonians.

So, before we can claim a Zion identity, we must first come out of Babylon, which represents the place of our spiritual captivity. This is where receiving the gospel message, restoring covenant with

God, getting delivered, and coming into fellowship with the righteous saints of God come in. You cannot live in Babylon and Zion at the same time. You must deliberately separate yourself from Babylon.

> And I heard another voice from heaven, saying, Come out of her, my people, that ye be not partakers of her sins, and that ye receive not of her plagues.
> —REVELATION 18:4

> Go ye forth of Babylon, flee ye from the Chaldeans, with a voice of singing declare ye, tell this, utter it even to the end of the earth; say ye, The LORD hath redeemed his servant Jacob.
> —ISAIAH 48:20

God does not desire for His people to remain in Babylon. Babylon is the city that is the direct opposite of Zion. Babylon is a place of weeping and captivity, while Zion is a place of joy and freedom. Babylon is a place of witchcraft, sorcery, and divination (magicians); Zion is a place of prophets and prophetic people. God redeemed His people from Babylon.

Babylon loves to take the best people. The king brought the best of the Israelites to Babylon. Daniel and the others were taught the language and knowledge of Babylon. (See Daniel 1.) Babylon is filled with worldly wisdom, but Zion has the wisdom of God. Babylon is worldly, carnal, and fleshly; Zion is spiritual and heavenly.

Babylon was a physical city, but it also represents something in the spirit. Babylonian systems are religious systems that do not allow people to enjoy the liberty of the Spirit.

Babylon is guilty of fornication and idolatry (Rev. 14:8). Babylon is a harlot (Rev. 17:5). Zion is a place of holiness and true worship; Babylon is a place of uncleanliness and demons. Zion is the place of glory!

God used Babylon to capture His people; then God judged Babylon for its pride and cruelty. Babylon is self-promoting; Zion is promoted by God. Babylon is legalistic; it is all about religious control, which it does through the traditions of men.

Babylonian leaders are controlling and domineering. They do not release and launch people into their destinies. Babylon loves to control the wealth; it is greedy and eats up the riches of the people. Zion, on the other hand, gives willingly and sacrificially.

Babylon is a place of sorrow. The psalmist said, "By the rivers of Babylon, there we sat down, yea, we wept, when we remembered Zion" (Ps. 137:1). Babylon is a place of rivers. Ezekiel had his visions by the river Chebar in Babylon (Ezek. 1:1). Darius, the Mede, captured Babylon by drying up the river and entering through the dry channel (Dan. 5:30–31). Both Zion and Babylon have rivers. But Zion has the life-giving river of God, whereas the rivers of Babylon do not give life.

After the Israelites had been in captivity for roughly seventy years, God restored them back to the land. He returned them to Zion, a place of freedom and protection from their enemies and a place of rebuilding and restoration after their deliverance. This is a type of what Jesus came to do. He came to bring restoration. In Zion the gospel is preached, and it liberates and sets free. It brings hope and deliverance. This is what the psalmist longed to see when he proclaimed, "Oh that the salvation of Israel were come out of Zion! When the Lord bringeth back the captivity of his people, Jacob shall rejoice, and Israel shall be glad" (Ps. 14:7).

As I mentioned, Zion is the opposite of Babylon. Zion is liberty; Babylon is bondage. The Zion believer cannot be satisfied in Babylon. Zion is laughter and joy; Babylon is weeping and sadness. Zion worships the true God; Babylon worships idols. Zion is divine order; Babylon is confusion. Zion is the home of the believer; Babylon represents exile.

LOOSE YOURSELF FROM BABYLON'S GRIP

According to Revelation 19:1–10, Babylon has been judged and is fallen. It no longer has dominion over Zion. Because the spiritual nature of Zion dwells in you, you are Zion. That means you are free. As Galatians 4:3–9 indicates, you are no longer in bondage to the elemental spirits or the weak and beggarly elements (man-made religious tradition or the philosophical teachings of the world). So stand fast in your liberty. Do not be entangled again with the yoke of bondage (Gal. 5:1). The Son has set you free, which means you are free indeed (John 8:36). Be glad and rejoice!

> When the LORD turned again the captivity of Zion, we were like them that dream. Then was our mouth filled with laughter, and our tongue with singing: then said they among the heathen, the LORD hath done great things for them. The LORD hath done great things for us; whereof we are glad.
> —PSALM 126:1–3

Zion believers belong in Zion churches. They do not belong in Babylonian systems. They cannot sit under control and domination. They need to be where their gifts are recognized and released. Thanks be to God that we don't have to live in Babylon.

Zion believers laugh and sing. The Lord's salvation has come. The Lord has done great things for us, and we are glad.

God commands Zion believers to come out of Babylon. Those with hearts after Zion will flee Babylon. They will loose themselves from Babylon's bonds and come into the freedom of Zion. If you want to experience the fullness of the glory of Zion in your life, you have to deliver yourself. Zechariah 2:7 says, "Deliver thyself, O Zion, that dwellest with the daughter of Babylon."

The Zion heart cannot stay in the dust. The call of Zion will cause the person to desire freedom. Zion shakes herself free. God said through the prophet Isaiah, "Shake thyself from the dust; arise, and sit down, O Jerusalem: loose thyself from the bands of thy neck, O captive daughter of Zion" (Isa. 52:2). God says loose thyself!

Zion awakes. Zion puts on strength. Zion puts on beautiful garments. The unclean cannot enter Zion, as Zion is for the holy and clean. The Zion identity is for those with clean hands and pure hearts.

> But Jerusalem which is above is free, which is the mother of us all.
> —Galatians 4:26

The church is heavenly Zion (Heb. 12:22–23), and the heavenly Zion is free. We are not slaves.

In Galatians 4:24–25 Zion is compared with Mount Sinai, which represents the law and legalism. Sinai is symbolized by Hagar, the bondwoman. And Galatians 4 tells us we are not born of the bondwoman but of the free (Zion).

The New Testament Pharisees had become legalistic. They were judgmental and hypocritical, and they brought the people into bondage through their teachings and traditions, many of which came out of Babylon (specifically the rabbinic writings collected in the Babylonian Talmud).[1] Jesus exposed and rebuked the Pharisees, knowing they were wicked and envious of Him. (See Mark 7:1–13.) Ultimately God called His people out of apostate Judaism into the church.

Babylon traffics in the souls of men (Rev. 18:13). No person or system should control your soul. Babylon hunts and trades in the souls of men (Ezek. 13:18), but our souls are as watered gardens in Zion (Jer. 31:12). Our souls are nourished in Zion instead of being enslaved in Babylon.

The Book of Revelation is a tale of two cities, Babylon and the New Jerusalem. Babylon is judged, and Jerusalem comes to the earth from heaven. Heavenly Jerusalem replaces fallen Babylon. Babylon is the city where the Lord was crucified (old Jerusalem), and it is also known as Sodom and Egypt (Rev. 11:8).

Moses brought the Israelites out of Egypt; God brought His people out of Babylon, and still today He brings us out of captivity so we can serve Him and live in the blessing and freedom that comes from serving Him. We do not serve Pharaoh or demons. We are Zion; we are servants of the Lord.

We cannot develop hearts after God without shedding our old desires and old ways. Deliverance and spiritual warfare are part of this process as much as the physical warfare and chastening from God were for the people of Israel. Zion believers have gone through this process and have an unshakable heart for God and the things of God. Just as God chooses Zion, the Zion believer chooses God.

When you understand the magnitude of Zion, how it is in you, how God inhabits Zion, and how it, therefore, inhabits you, everything you touch will prosper. Every place you go you will be favored, blessed, and promoted. The glory of God dwells in Zion. The glory of God dwells in you.

GOD'S DWELLING PLACE

When we go back into the Old Testament and study what happened during the old covenant, there was a point when the tribes of Israel were moving into Canaan. The question then became, "Which area will God choose to be His dwelling place?" At this time in their journey, the children of Israel had been carrying the presence of God in the ark of the covenant, which God commanded Moses to make in Exodus 25. The ark was an earthly replica of the ark in heaven. The ark represents the throne of God in the earth and is referred to by many titles in the Old Testament, such as:

+ the ark of the testimony (Exod. 25:22)

+ the ark of the covenant of the Lord (Num. 10:33)

+ the ark of the Lord God (1 Kings 2:26)

+ the ark of the Lord, the Lord of all the earth (Josh. 3:13)

+ the ark of God (1 Sam. 3:3)

+ the holy ark (2 Chron. 35:3)

+ the ark of thy strength (Ps. 132:8)

+ the ark of the covenant of God (Judg. 20:27)

+ the ark of the covenant (Josh. 3:6)

+ the ark of the Lord (Josh. 4:11)

+ the ark of the God of Israel (1 Sam. 5:7)

+ the ark of acacia wood (Exod. 25:10, nkjv)

The tabernacle the people of Israel carried through the wilderness was in a place called Shiloh, but that was not God's chosen place. It was temporary. We know they brought the ark out of the tabernacle of Moses. Then they went into battle with the Philistines and lost possession of the ark. (See 1 Samuel 4:5–11.) For a time the Philistines had possession of the ark, and God sent plagues on them until they returned the ark (1 Sam. 6; 7:1–2).

The land had been divided among the twelve tribes into twelve areas. Which area would God choose? The choice was not made until David became king.

From the time of Joshua until the time of David, there was no specific place that God had yet revealed as His dwelling place. Yes, the people had come out of the wilderness—and all the first generation except Joshua and Caleb died out there. Yes, the new generation had come into the land of Canaan, the Promised Land, which is considered good land. But Zion is an entirely different place—Zion is the place God has chosen for Himself.

Since the time of Israel, Zion has transcended the natural, physical realm into being a spiritual place and state of the heart. *I Am Zion* is the result of many years of preaching and studying the subject of Zion. These messages have changed my life in many ways, and as I present them to you, I believe these messages will change your life as well. A revelation of Zion is a key to understanding much of Scripture and the purpose of God for the church and the world. Many truths are connected to Zion, and I am still learning and discovering new facets of the great city.

The word Zion is used more than 150 times in the King James Version of the Bible. "It essentially means 'fortification' and carries the idea of being 'raised up' as a 'monument.'"[2] From its first mention in 2 Samuel 5, the word Zion expands in scope and takes on an additional, spiritual meaning as the Scriptures progress.[3] The psalms are filled with references to Zion, which is not surprising considering that Zion is also called the city of David. The word Zion also refers to Jerusalem, and the two terms are often used interchangeably.

In Scripture there are two Zions. There is the earthly Zion—Jerusalem, the place where God dwelled—and then there was the heavenly Zion written about in the New Testament and that comes as a fulfillment of the earthly Zion. Ancient Israel was part of the earthly Zion, but as children of God we are part of the heavenly Zion.

The heavenly Jerusalem is greater than the earthly, and we have come to the heavenly, which is described in Psalm 48.

> Great is the Lord, and greatly to be praised in the city of our God, in the mountain of his holiness. Beautiful for situation, the joy of the whole earth, is mount Zion, on the sides of the north, the city of the great King.
>
> —Psalm 48:1–2

Zion is "the joy of the whole earth," and indeed it is one of the most important places and symbols in Scripture. But it is important to keep it at the front of our hearts and minds as we study this revelation that Zion is more than a location. The physical Zion is a type, shadow, or symbol of both the corporate church and the individual believer. Jerusalem was the place where the temple was housed. It was the place where God dwelled. But under the new covenant and because of Christ, God dwells in us. The church is the body of Christ; we are His dwelling place. Therefore we are Zion, both corporately and individually.

A Zion Identity

At one point some years ago when I had just come into the revelation of Zion, I would emphasize that we, the church, are corporate Zion. But recently I have come to understand that the individual believer is also Zion. Zion is the city of God, and in the Sermon on the Mount, Jesus likened you as a believer to a city. He said, "Ye are the light of the world. A *city* that is set on an *hill* cannot be hid" (Matt. 5:14, emphasis added). The Bible also says in Proverbs 25:28, "He that hath no rule over his own spirit is like a *city* that is broken down, and without walls" (emphasis added). Zion was once known as the city of David and the city of God—the place where God dwelled. We are likened unto a city within which God dwells—a city of lights that cannot be hidden. That light is the glory of God, which will we come to know as the glory of Zion.

Zion is a place of rule, reign, and dominion; it is a picture of the kingdom. Zion's walls are strong. They are made of jasper and other precious jewels, and the city is a stronghold upheld by God. It is a place of authority and power. As you are saved and delivered from the hand of the enemy, the glory of Zion restores you and rebuilds your walls. You are no longer vulnerable to attack. You are strong and fortified, as Zion is.

Under the old covenant Zion was merely a location, but now it is a people. You are Zion. Christ, who is the spiritual nature of Zion, dwells in you and every other believer. When you receive Christ, you will get a full measure of the benefits of salvation. You can experience a whole new life as a Zion believer. Because of Christ you can declare, "I am Zion." You are that glorious city set on a hill. You are a stronghold and fortress for the righteousness of God. You are a person of power, authority, and dominion as you rule and reign with Christ.

Every chapter in this book builds from the foundation of types and shadows of the physical place called Zion and expands it into the spiritual reality of it as it has been made full and complete in Christ. Throughout our study I will refer to the body of Christ at large for context, but my emphasis will be on you, the individual believer.

My prayer for you is that you will come into an understanding of Zion that will expand your understanding of what it means to be in Christ. I believe this revelation will help you walk in the fullness of who you are in Him. I have a desire to see believers walk in their identity because your identity determines your destiny. Do you know who you are? Do you know who you are in Christ? A proper identity is key to being who God has called you to be. The Scripture reveals who we are in Christ, but it takes a revelation from heaven to truly see and know it. I pray that you receive the spirit of wisdom and revelation as you read the pages of this book.

I Am Zion Confessions

God calls me Zion. I will not see myself the way others see me.

Zion is my name.

I am Zion, and God lives in me.

The enemy cannot defeat me, because God lives inside of me.

I receive my new identity. I am ready for things to change in my life.

I declare that I will go from poverty to prosperity.

I will be blessed with abundant provision and satisfied with food.

My provision is blessed.

No more poverty for my life. I will have abundant provision because I am Zion.

There is no lack in Zion. Zion has more than enough.

I am Zion. I have more than enough.

Glory rests on my life. I walk in abundance and blessing. God has chosen me, and whatever God chooses, He blesses.

I am ready for increase. I am ready for expansion. I am ready for enlargement. I will not stay small.

I will stick with Zion. I will not leave Zion. I will not walk away from Zion. I will stay with Zion. I will not be moved.

I will stay with the glory of Zion. I will not be distracted.

Zion is God's place. I will stay in God's place.

I will arise.

I am Zion.

YOU ARE ZION, THE CITY OF GOD

Zion, the heavenly city,
The earthly was a type.
The city of God,
The place of rule and reign.

John saw the city come down,
Filled with the glory of God.
The gates are always opened.
The nations are invited to come.

The river of God flows.
This river brings life.
It makes glad the city of God,
The tabernacles of the Most High.

Zion, the place of worship,
The church of the living God,
The place of glory and beauty,
And the place of commanded blessing.

God has chosen Zion,
His habitation forever.
Many are born in Zion,
Their names recorded in the book.

Zion, a stronghold,
No enemy can defeat.
A place of towers and bulwarks,
The city of the King.

The saints gather in Zion,
They offer to the King high praise,
Zion, a city of worshippers,
A city of kings and priests.

Zion, the place of dominion,
The place of power and authority,
The place of ruling and reigning,
And the place of liberty.

Zion, a high place,
It knows the joy of victory.
Zion, the heavenly place,
Saints' names recorded in the book.

God has a city.
Zion is that place.
The mountain of His holiness.
The place of great praise.

There is a river
Whose streams make the city glad.
This river flows in Zion,
The city of our God.

His kingdom citizens reside there.
It is their residence.
They abide in that place,
Zion, the city of God.

Zion, a city in Judah,
The tribe of praise.
Zion, the high place,
The city above all.

Those with Zion hearts,
Those who love the city of God,
They shout to the God of glory
And lift their voices on high.

The city of God is a fortress.
Saints dwell there in safety.
No weapon can prosper against her.
Her enemies must bow.

Come to Zion and worship.
Come to Zion and abide.
This is the city of God,
The dwelling place of the Most High.

Chapter 1

THE STRONGHOLD OF ZION

Nevertheless David took the strong hold of
Zion: the same is the city of David.
—2 Samuel 5:7

THE CITY OF Zion was a stronghold, a fortress, held by the Jebusites, and David conquered this stronghold and made it his city, the base from which he led the nation of Israel. From this point on Zion would take a central role in the nation of Israel.

Before David captured the city, the Jebusites taunted him, saying the blind and lame would keep him from entering their citadel. They considered it impenetrable. Nevertheless David took their stronghold by sending men through the water tunnel to infiltrate the city. (See 2 Samuel 5.) The conquest became the first in a series of victories for David, and it signaled a turning point in the young king's life, as it solidified his rule and reign over the region.

Through this victory Zion was transformed from being the fortress of the Jebusites to being David's fortress. As I mentioned previously, the old covenant is a series of types and shadows of the new covenant we have through Christ. And so with Israel's possessing this new territory comes the foundational types and shadows of the gospel and the kingdom of God. David is a type and picture of Christ, as Jesus is called the son of David (Matt. 1:1). And the city of David, as it is called in the verse above, is a type and picture of the city of God. The Scriptures have much to say about the city of God. It is where God dwells—the place of His rule and reign and the seat of His dominion and power. It is God's fortress. The psalmist declared:

> Great is the LORD, and greatly to be praised in the city of our God, in the mountain of his holiness. Beautiful for situation, the joy of the whole earth, is mount Zion, on the sides of the north, the city of the great King.
> —PSALM 48:1–2

Zion is "beautiful for situation." This means literally that it is beautiful for elevation. Zion is an elevated place, which represents its preeminence and prominence. As the previous passage points out, Zion is "on the sides of the north." When we think of north, we point or look up. Zion is up on the north side, signifying its loftiness and distinction. Zion is above all other cities.

As we understand that the spiritual nature of Zion dwells in us, we gain a more complete revelation of our spiritual position in Christ. The physical Zion was situated in a lofty place, and we, the spiritual Zion, are seated in heavenly places in Christ (Eph. 2:6). We have been exalted through Christ above principalities and powers. We are not under the rule of Satan; we are to rule over him. Zion people are people of power and authority.

In the Book of Psalms Zion is described as having towers, palaces, and bulwarks.

> Walk about Zion, and go round about her: tell the towers thereof. Mark ye well her bulwarks, consider her palaces; that ye may tell it to the generation following. For this God is our God for ever and ever: he will be our guide even unto death.
> —PSALM 48:12–14

Palaces, in this passage, is literally referring to citadels.[1] A citadel is a fortress, typically on high ground, protecting or dominating a city. Towers and bulwarks are symbols of strength, power, and fortification. *Fortify* means "to strengthen and secure (a place, such as a town)" with defensive works such as forts or batteries so it will be protected against attack.[2] We see a clearer picture of the strength of Zion's bulwarks and towers in *The Message* Bible's paraphrase of Psalm 48:12–14: "Circle Zion, take her measure, count her fortress peaks, gaze long at her sloping bulwark, climb her citadel heights."

Zion was fortified by its towers. These are elevated places of defense and safety that were used by watchmen. Although the towers around the physical Zion were made of stone, an individual can also be a tower and a fortress. Intercessors and prophets stand on the watchtower, serving as guardians and protectors, as we see in the following scriptures:

> I have set thee for a tower and a fortress among my people, that thou mayest know and try their way.
>
> —JEREMIAH 6:27

> And thou, O tower of the flock, the strong hold of the daughter of Zion, unto thee shall it come, even the first dominion; the kingdom shall come to the daughter of Jerusalem.
>
> —MICAH 4:8

YOU ARE A STRONGHOLD FOR GOD

Do you consider yourself Zion? Do you consider yourself a tower? Do you consider yourself a stronghold? As you come into the revelation that you are Zion, you will understand that you are also a stronghold for God. You are a strong tower through Christ. You are a fortress, a guardian, and a protector.

A bulwark is a solid wall-like structure—strong support or protection.[3] Zion is well defended because of its towers and bulwarks, and this is how we should see the church and the individual believer. You are a city set on a hill that is well defended with towers and bulwarks. You are a strong city through Christ. Begin to see yourself this way. Confess this with your mouth. You are not weak. You are strong in Christ. You are built up through the Word and the Spirit.

Zion is built upon Christ. He supports and holds it up, meaning He supports you and holds you up. Isaiah prophesied:

> Therefore thus saith the Lord God, Behold, I lay in Zion for a foundation a stone, a tried stone, a precious corner stone, a sure foundation: he that believeth shall not make haste.
> —Isaiah 28:16

Zion no longer has a physical foundation. Jesus is the foundation of Zion, and He is the foundation of your life and of the church. God declared in Isaiah 51:16:

> And I have put my words in thy mouth, and I have covered thee in the shadow of mine hand, that I may plant the heavens, and lay the foundations of the earth, and say unto Zion, Thou art my people.

Zion, which was a physical place, is now a people. God is more concerned about people than physical places. The physical in the old covenant was a type and picture of something spiritual under the new covenant. Zion becomes the new creation, the church. Zion is the believer, the new creature.

The foundation supports the structure. The larger the structure, the greater the foundation. Zion is a great city. Psalm 87:3 says, "Glorious things are spoken of thee, O city of God. Selah." The Good News Translation says it this way: "Listen, city of God, to the wonderful things he says about you." God does great things in Zion, and He does great things for you.

I have a passion to speak about the glorious truths of Zion because they apply to the believer. There is greatness in Zion, and you possess greatness as a believer in Christ. God commands us to open our ears and listen. God is speaking to us. He wants us to hear the glorious and wonderful things He has to say about us.

Psalm 48 says in verses 4–6:

> For, lo, the kings were assembled, they passed by together. They saw it, and so they marvelled; they were troubled, and

hasted away. Fear took hold upon them there, and pain, as of a woman in travail.

This is what the enemy feels when he sees Zion. The enemy marvels. The enemy is troubled. The enemy runs away in fear, and pain comes upon him as of a woman in travail.

Other translations say the kings were astonished and awe-struck when they saw Zion. When they looked at the great city, they froze with fear and fled in terror. The Passion Translation says when the mighty kings who united to oppose Zion "saw God manifest in front of their eyes, they were stunned. Trembling, they all fled away, gripped with fear. Seized with panic, they doubled up in frightful anguish like a woman in the labor pains of childbirth" (Ps. 48:4–6).

You Are the Strength and Beauty of Zion

In the description from Psalm 48 Zion is a picture of strength and beauty. According to Psalm 50:2, Zion is the perfection of beauty. As Zion dwells in you, you too have the strength and beauty of God.

God is a God of beauty. It is an attribute of His glory. David desired to "behold the beauty of the Lord" (Ps. 27:4), and we worship in the beauty of holiness (Ps. 96:9). God's beauty is upon us (Ps. 90:17). God is our crown of glory and diadem of beauty (Isa. 28:5). God gives us beauty for ashes (Isa. 61:3), and strength and beauty are in God's sanctuary (Ps. 96:6). Job 40:10 says, "Deck thyself now with majesty and excellency; and array thyself with glory and beauty." A loss of beauty is a loss of glory (Lam. 1:6). Zion is told to put on beautiful garments (Isa. 52:1), and as the spiritual dwelling place of Zion, you wear the beauty of the Lord.

Like the earthly Zion, heavenly Zion also is pictured with attributes of beauty. Revelation 21:18–20 says the foundations of the wall of the city were garnished with precious stones, which again represent glory and beauty:

And the building of the wall of it was of jasper: and the city was pure gold, like unto clear glass. And the foundations of the wall of the city were garnished with all manner of precious stones. The first foundation was jasper; the second, sapphire; the third, a chalcedony; the fourth, an emerald; the fifth, sardonyx; the sixth, sardius; the seventh, chrysolyte; the eighth, beryl; the ninth, a topaz; the tenth, a chrysoprasus; the eleventh, a jacinth; the twelfth, an amethyst.

Zion, the city of the King, is adorned in beauty, and the King rules and reigns from this place of glory and strength. David ruled from the physical Zion, and the King of kings, Jesus, rules and reigns in your life.

With Jesus as the head, Zion can't help but be victorious. All who attack Zion experience defeat because Zion cannot be defeated. This is how you must view yourself. Zion is a picture of the kingdom, and Jesus said, "The kingdom of God is within you" (Luke 17:21). Don't allow the enemy to intimidate you. You are victorious. You are a fortress. You are a citadel. You are the city of God—the city of the great King. God defends His city, which means He defends you.

The Lord is great in Zion. Its enemies tremble before Zion, and it "breakest the ships of Tarshish with an east wind" (Ps. 48:7). The ships of Tarshish represent a fleet or an armada, which are symbols of strength and power. The enemy's power is broken through Zion, meaning the enemy's power is broken through your life.

PUT ON THE STRENGTH OF ZION

Awake, awake; put on thy strength, O Zion; put on thy beautiful garments, O Jerusalem, the holy city: for henceforth there shall no more come into thee the uncircumcised and the unclean.

—ISAIAH 52:1

Zion is a strong city, and the Zion believer is also strong. Zion has walls and bulwarks of salvation. Zion sings the new song. The

Zion believer has a circumcised heart, and the uncircumcised and unclean cannot enter.

Because Zion sings strength and you are Zion, you sing strength.

> In that day shall this song be sung in the land of Judah; we have a strong city; salvation will God appoint for walls and bulwarks.
>
> —ISAIAH 26:1

You have the river of God flowing from your life. The river is filled with gladness.

> There is a river, the streams whereof shall make glad the city of God, the holy place of the tabernacles of the most High.
>
> —PSALM 46:4

We give God great praise in the city of God. The Names of God Bible translation of Psalm 48:1 says, "Yahweh is great. He should be highly praised."

> Great is the LORD, and greatly to be praised in the city of our God, in the mountain of his holiness.
>
> —PSALM 48:1

Zion is the city of the Lord of hosts (armies).

> As we have heard, so have we seen in the city of the LORD of hosts, in the city of our God: God will establish it for ever. Selah.
>
> —PSALM 48:8

> Glorious things are spoken of thee, O city of God. Selah.
>
> —PSALM 87:3

RECEIVE THE SHALOM OF ZION

Zion is the place of shalom, the peace of God. It is the stronghold of God, where there is no hurt or spiritual abuse. The wolf and the lamb dwell together. Jews and Gentiles are made one in Christ. People from all nations come to Zion to live in peace and enjoy undisturbed composure.

They shall not hurt nor destroy in all my holy mountain: for the earth shall be full of the knowledge of the LORD, as the waters cover the sea.

—Isaiah 11:9

The wolf and the lamb shall feed together, and the lion shall eat straw like the bullock: and dust shall be the serpent's meat. They shall not hurt nor destroy in all my holy mountain, saith the LORD.

—Isaiah 65:25

As Zion, the dwelling place of God, the peace of God resides in your heart and mind (Phil. 4:7). Nothing that is unlike God is allowed in Zion. As it was for the physical Zion, no strangers shall pass through our spiritual Zion. Only kingdom citizens can live in this city and maintain a heart after Zion.

So shall ye know that I am the LORD your God dwelling in Zion, my holy mountain: then shall Jerusalem be holy, and there shall no strangers pass through her any more.

—Joel 3:17

Zion is heavenly. Zion is a heavenly people living on the earth. The kingdom is heaven coming to the earth. The mountain of the Lord fills the earth.

And he carried me away in the spirit to a great and high mountain, and shewed me that great city, the holy Jerusalem, descending out of heaven from God.

—Revelation 21:10

LET THE REDEMPTION OF ZION COME INTO YOUR LIFE

To appoint unto them that mourn in Zion, to give unto them beauty for ashes, the oil of joy for mourning, the garment of praise for the spirit of heaviness; that they might be called trees of righteousness, the planting of the LORD, that he might be glorified.

—ISAIAH 61:3

Zion went into mourning because of disobedience. But Jesus came to redeem Zion and give beauty for ashes, which represent defeat and sorrow. The glory restores beauty. Zion is beautiful because the glory of the Lord is there. You are Zion, and that means you are beautiful.

The glory also restores joy. In Zion we receive joy and gladness instead of depression and defeat. We receive the garment of praise and display the splendor of the Lord. Isaiah 61 says we would be called "trees of righteousness, the planting of the LORD, that he might be glorified." We receive the oil of joy for the spirit of heaviness. Zion is the place of joy and gladness. As we take on a Zion identity, God will deliver us from depression and defeat. We will receive the garment of praise.

In this verse we also learn that as Zion believers we are trees of righteousness. We are the planting of the Lord. Isaiah 60, which I call the glory chapter, speaks about trees. The glory is typified by Lebanon. Lebanon is a nation of magnificent trees. God is glorified in Zion because He is glorified through us. We are Zion.

Now that we understand what and who Zion is, let's go deeper into understanding how it has become God's choice, His desire, and His dwelling place or habitation forever.

Chapter 2

THE HABITATION OF GOD

For the LORD hath chosen Zion; he hath desired
it for his habitation. This is my rest for ever:
here will I dwell; for I have desired it.
—PSALM 132:13–14

GOD HAS ALWAYS desired to dwell among His people. Since the days of the tabernacle of Moses, God has made it clear He wants to make His habitation among His people. But it was not until the establishment of the earthly Zion that the pattern for how God would dwell among us took on eternal implications. To see this progression, let's go back a few hundred years before the occupation of Zion to the time just after Moses had made the tabernacle according to God's specifications, when the people of Israel were making their way into the Promised Land.

SHILOH

After journeying in the wilderness, the people of Israel, under the leadership of Joshua, crossed over into the Promised Land, which was Canaan. If you remember, Moses, who led them out of Egypt, was not permitted to enter the Promised Land because he "broke faith with [God] in the presence of the Israelites at the waters of Meribah Kadesh" and because he "did not uphold [God's] holiness among the Israelites" (Deut. 32:51, NIV). So Joshua, who had exhibited great faith in God and courage (see Numbers 14), took the tabernacle of Moses, which contained the ark of God, and brought it into the Promised Land. Once there the tabernacle was set up in Shiloh.

Shiloh is where Hannah prayed for a son and made a vow to the Lord. (See 1 Samuel 1–2.) Shiloh is also the place where the young prophet Samuel, the son for whom Hannah prayed, heard the voice of God. Shiloh is where Eli mentored and raised up young Samuel. It is also where Eli's sons, Hophni and Phinehas, were wicked and corrupt priests. (See 1 Samuel 2:12–25.) They despised the holy things of God and eventually brought judgment upon the house of Eli.

For a moment, however, Shiloh was the place where the tabernacle, the ark of God, and His presence dwelled. And for a moment Shiloh was the place God made His habitation among the people.

Unfortunately the moment wouldn't last long. Joshua died and "another generation grew up who knew neither the LORD nor what he had done for Israel. Then the Israelites did evil in the eyes of the LORD and served the Baals. They forsook the LORD, the God of their ancestors, who had brought them out of Egypt. They followed and worshiped various gods of the peoples around them. They aroused the LORD's anger" (Judg. 2:10–12, NIV).

They did not honor God. They did not seek His presence. They rebelled against Him and did what was right in their own eyes (Judg. 21:25). So God "forsook the tabernacle of Shiloh, the tent He had placed among men, and delivered His strength into captivity, and His glory into the enemy's hand" (Ps. 78:60–61, NKJV).

This is around the time when the Philistines took the ark, which was one of the most tragic defeats for Israel. They presumed the ark would assure them victory if they brought it into battle with them:

> And when the people were come into the camp, the elders of Israel said, Wherefore hath the LORD smitten us to day before the Philistines? Let us fetch the ark of the covenant of the LORD out of Shiloh unto us, that, when it cometh among us, it may save us out of the hand of our enemies.

> So the people sent to Shiloh, that they might bring from
> thence the ark of the covenant of the LORD of hosts, which
> dwelleth between the cherubims: and the two sons of Eli,
> Hophni and Phinehas, were there with the ark of the cov-
> enant of God.
>
> And when the ark of the covenant of the LORD came into
> the camp, all Israel shouted with a great shout, so that the
> earth rang again.
>
> —1 SAMUEL 4:3–5

As it turns out, what they thought was a good strategy was not.
They lost the battle and the ark. The sons of Eli were slain (this,
of course, was God's judgment against them for their abomina-
tions). Upon hearing the news, Eli fell and broke his neck, and his
daughter-in-law went into travail with child (vv. 18–19). She named
her child Ichabod, meaning the glory is departed from Israel (v. 22).

We know the ark of God represents His glory, so when the ark
departs, so does the glory. Israel was ordained to be the keepers
of the ark. They were chosen by God to be blessed with His presence. No other nation had that privilege. The Philistines were not
ordained to be keepers of the ark, so when they brought the ark to
their land, they suffered tremendous judgments from God.

The ark of God would never return to Shiloh. It would not be
until David set up his tabernacle that the presence of God would
return to dwell among the people.

RECAPTURING THE ARK OF GOD

With the ark of God in their possession the Philistines experienced heavy judgment from God (see 1 Samuel 5–6), so much so
that they arranged with the Israelite army to return it. This was
during the reign of King Saul. And for twenty years of his reign
the ark remained in Kirjath-jearim. When David became king, it
was his first order of business to bring the ark back to Israel. He
wanted it near him. He knew that having it in his city, near his
throne, would mean blessing, protection, and the presence of God.

Once David had taken the stronghold of Zion and established it as his city, his fortress, David set out to recover the ark.

His first attempt to move the ark ended in failure with the death of Uzzah (2 Sam. 6:7). So he carried the ark aside into the house of Obededom, where it remained for three months. God blessed the house of Obededom because of the ark (2 Sam. 6:10–11). David saw the blessing that came upon the household of Obededom and desired to have the ark reside in his city even more, so he made a second and final attempt to move the ark. This time he was successful.

> And it was told king David, saying, The LORD hath blessed the house of Obededom, and all that pertaineth unto him, because of the ark of God. So David went and brought up the ark of God from the house of Obededom into the city of David with gladness. And it was so, that when they that bare the ark of the LORD had gone six paces, he sacrificed oxen and fatlings. And David danced before the LORD with all his might; and David was girded with a linen ephod. So David and all the house of Israel brought up the ark of the LORD with shouting, and with the sound of the trumpet.
> —2 SAMUEL 6:12–15

This was a time of great celebration in Israel, and as I'll discuss in a later chapter, Zion would become a picture of praise and rejoicing. The psalmist wrote, "Let mount Zion rejoice, let the daughters of Judah be glad, because of thy judgments" (Ps. 48:11).

David entered Zion with shouts of praise because the ark would reside there. The ark was the most valuable piece of furniture in Israel. It was placed in the most holy place between the cherubim (2 Chron. 5:7), and the glory of God rested upon it. The ark was a picture of God's presence and glory, and it represented the strength and power of God (Ps. 132:8). When the ark came to Zion, it became God's habitation, and as God's habitation it became the place of God's strength. What's even greater than the ark being

14

brought to Zion is that Zion was also the place God chose for Himself to dwell forever.

> For the LORD hath chosen Zion; he hath desired it for his habitation. This is my rest *for ever*: here will I dwell; for I have desired it. I will abundantly bless her provision: I will satisfy her poor with bread. I will also clothe her priests with salvation: and her saints shall shout aloud for joy. There will I make the horn of David to bud: I have ordained a lamp for mine anointed. His enemies will I clothe with shame: but upon himself shall his crown flourish.
>
> —PSALM 132:13–18, EMPHASIS ADDED

It is important to note here that while David placed the ark of God under a tent in Zion, the tabernacle of Moses was still in Shiloh. As I pointed out above, the presence of God left Shiloh. God forsook it (Ps. 78:60). He removed His presence from that place. He chose instead the tribe of Judah and Zion (Ps. 78:68).

This is an important transition. Rather than dwell in the midst of animal sacrifices (Shiloh), God now chose to dwell in the midst of praise (Zion). The Lord loved the gates of Zion more than all the dwellings (tabernacles) of Jacob. He loved them because the praise and worship ordained by David around the ark manifested the same atmosphere of worship found in heaven. Zion was the earthly expression of the heavenly worship in which God continually dwells. God therefore "inhabited" the praises of earthly Zion just as He dwells in the worship of the heavenlies. (See Psalm 22:3.)

Do you see why we must get this revelation of Zion? If we want God to dwell among us, if we want to know His power in our lives, and if we want His glory, we must come to know ourselves and the church as the spiritual dwelling place of God. We are Zion. God has always desired to dwell within and among His people. We can align our hearts with His desire and come into the fullness of this understanding and see the majesty, beauty, and glory of God in our midst!

How God Kept His "Zion Forever" Promise

David's reign over the people of Israel was prosperous, though he experienced many failures. He was known as the man after God's heart. Yet God would not allow David to fulfill the prophecy that he would build the temple at Jerusalem, which would become the permanent physical dwelling place for the ark. Instead the task would be passed on to his son Solomon, who did indeed build the temple in Jerusalem (1 Kings 6:1–6). But if you remember, Solomon disobeyed God and married foreign wives who worshipped foreign gods. This led Solomon to serve these gods or idols as well (1 Kings 11:1–4).

In judgment against Solomon's actions God tore the kingdom from Solomon and split it in two. He gave ten tribes, called the northern tribes, to a general by the name of Jeroboam, and the two southern tribes—Judah and Benjamin—to Solomon's son Rehoboam. To read the biblical account of this judgment and the order of rule established after it, see 1 Kings 11–12.

God did not take the entire kingdom away from Solomon because He had promised David that David's seed would sit on the throne of Israel forever. Of course, "forever" has been culminated with Jesus being the son of David. God, in His mercy, preserved two tribes for David's descendants, but He took ten tribes and gave them to Jeroboam. Israel was split into the southern kingdom, which is called Judah, and the northern kingdom, which is called Israel. Jesus is how God has kept His promise that He would make Zion His habitation and rest forever.

Jesus, the One who came through the line of David, conquered death and sits on the throne of the heavenly Zion forever. This is why Zion can no longer be limited simply to a physical place. Christ reigns in our hearts (Rom. 8:10; 2 Cor. 13:5; Gal. 2:20; Eph. 3:17), within which is His kingdom (Luke 17:21—"the kingdom of God is within you"), and He reigns in heavenly Zion forever:

He will be great and eminent and will be called the Son of the Most High; and the Lord God will give Him the throne of His father David; and He will reign over the house of Jacob (Israel) forever, and of His kingdom there shall be no end.

—Luke 1:32–33, amp

We Don't Choose; God Does

During the time of Judah, many kings in Solomon's line were evil. There were a few who were good, such as Asa, Jehoshaphat, Hezekiah, Ahaziah, and Josiah, but eventually God took Judah into Babylonian captivity. (See Jeremiah 39–43.)

The northern kingdom, on the other hand, never had one good king. Every king in the north was rebellious, beginning with Jeroboam and his descendants on through Ahab and Jezebel and others. God took the kingdom from him. Before this, God had given Jeroboam a prophetic word that God was taking ten tribes of Israel and giving them to him (1 Kings 11:30–31). But God had also commanded that all twelve tribes of Israel were to go to Jerusalem three times a year to worship—Passover, Pentecost, and Tabernacles.[1] Even though God split the nation, He still expected all the tribes to come together in Jerusalem to worship and then return home to their respective territories.

But Jeroboam was afraid that if the tribes he ruled went to Jerusalem to worship, they would defect from him. In 2 Kings 12:26–33, we read that Jeroboam set up two places for the people to worship that God did not ordain. He established false priesthoods—one in Dan and the other in Bethel. These two places became places of false worship. He told the ten tribes, "It is too much for you to go up to Jerusalem. Here are your gods, O Israel, which brought you up from the land of Egypt!" (v. 28, nkjv). A false priesthood, which Jeroboam "devised in his own heart" (v. 33, nkjv), was established.

Regardless of what Jeroboam tried to establish, God had ordained that Jerusalem, or Zion, was the place of worship. Jeroboam was in rebellion. He didn't even get in there to rule, but immediately he pulled the people of Israel away from the true God and into false worship, all because he didn't trust God. Even though God had given him a prophetic word, he was afraid they would defect from him and return to Jerusalem. He needed to trust that when God gives a person something, it will be blessed. The blessing of God comes with no sorrow attached. Jeroboam could have trusted that God would be faithful to His Word. But he didn't. I believe God would have allowed Jeroboam to remain ruler over the land if he would have allowed the people to go to Jerusalem and then return to their homes in the northern kingdom. Instead Jeroboam tried to override the eternal choice of God, which is always Zion.

God was very serious about the people honoring His chosen place of worship. Often, when the psalmists would sing and prophesy, they would declare to Israel that the true place of worship is Zion. They would prophesy that Zion is the place God has chosen. Zion is the place of His habitation, not these other places where the northern tribes were going. Yet, despite those who followed Jeroboam's directive, there were still people faithful to come from the north all the way to Jerusalem. There is always a remnant. Even though Jeroboam told them not to come, there were some who still came because they knew the places he had established were false.

As judgment against Jeroboam's rebellion against the Lord's instructions, the northern kingdom went into captivity many years before the southern kingdom. God sent the Assyrians to take them captive (2 Kings 17). The headquarters of Assyria was Nineveh. This is why Jonah did not want to go preach in Nineveh—he did not like the Assyrians as they were the enemies of Israel.[2] The Assyrians came, and the ten northern tribes were swallowed up. This is how the northern kingdom became known as the lost tribes of Israel.

Sennacherib, who was the king of Assyria, attempted to take Judah, the southern kingdom, as well during the reign of Hezekiah

(2 Kings 18:13). Hezekiah called upon God (2 Kings 19:14–19), and God answered Hezekiah. Because Hezekiah trusted God, God sent an angel and killed 185,000 Assyrians in one day (2 Kings 19:35), so Jerusalem did not go into captivity at that time. The kingdom of Judah was extended for a number of years. It had a few more revivals, the one during the reign of Josiah being the last, and finally God took the southern kingdom into Babylon.[3]

Often when you read the psalms, they'll emphasize Zion, Jerusalem, the place of God's blessing, the place of God's glory, the place of God's habitation, and the place of true worship, to let Israel know they could not go to these false places. They must come to the place God had chosen.

Even today we can't just pick and choose how we're going to worship God. The Bible says they who worship God must worship Him in spirit and in truth. (See John 4:24.) We just can't pick and choose and say, "I think I'll be a Buddhist." "I think I'll be a Hindu." "I think I'll be a Muslim." "I think I'll be a Mormon." "I will just pick a religion I like, and I will worship the way I like."

No, it's not up to you to choose the way you worship. God has chosen Zion. Zion has always been God's place of worship. Zion has always been the place where His presence dwells. Zion has always been the place of glory. As we know, it is the place where God dwells, the place where God inhabits. It's a place of prosperity, blessing, and abundance. Why? Because God is there.

UNDERSTANDING FOREVER

Notice that God says in Psalm 132:14, "This is my rest *for ever*: here will I dwell" (emphasis added). The word *forever* brings us to the eternal aspect of Zion. Anytime you see the word *forever* in the Old Testament, it can mean two different things. It can mean a long period, or it can represent an age. It is a Hebrew word, *ad*, which means "perpetuity, forever, continuing future," "everlasting," "eternity," "perpetually."[4] The picture is a horizon for as far as you can see.

19

God told Israel He would choose Aaron and his descendants as priests forever (Exod. 40:15). The Hebrew word used as *forever* in this instance is *owlam,* which means "long duration," "ancient time," or "long time (of past)."[5]

The priesthood of Aaron ended. When the temple was destroyed and the old covenant was fulfilled, God initiated a greater priesthood called the Melchizedek priesthood. We no longer have an Aaronic priesthood because we no longer need it. We no longer need men to bring animal sacrifices to a temple. That was the primary priestly responsibility of Aaron and his sons. When that system was over, it ended—even though God said, "I made it a statute forever." (See Exod. 27:21, NKJV.) *Forever* can mean the end of the age. In Young's Literal Translation it says "age-during" (Exod. 40:15). The word *forever* is translated from the Greek as "age-during," or until the end of the age, the end of that old covenant age.

The same thing is true with circumcision. God said the covenant of circumcision was forever, but it was an age-during right. It was to the end of the age. We no longer have to be circumcised in the flesh. We're now circumcised in the heart.

Also these things were types, shadows, and pictures of something greater to come. Physical Jerusalem, physical Zion, the physical temple where they went three times a year, was a picture of something heavenly, something that was coming. It was only a type and a shadow until Jesus came. When Jesus comes, He brings in the heavenly, the reality of what the type and symbol represents.

Earthly Jerusalem, earthly Zion, the earthly city, and the earthly temple were only a picture of a heavenly Jerusalem, heavenly Zion, heavenly temple, and heavenly city we see in the Book of Revelation coming down from heaven. It's something heavenly. The earth was first, the natural first, and then the spiritual, so it is forever. (See 1 Corinthians 15:46.)

God has an eternal Zion, but it's not an earthly city. It's a heavenly city. It's the city with foundations that Abraham looked unto—a city whose builder and maker is the Lord (Heb. 11:10; cf. Rev. 21:2, 14).

God wants us to know Zion is always the place where He dwells. If you want to find God, you need to find Zion. Where is Zion? It's not a physical or earthly place. It's something spiritual. Where is Zion? It's the place where God dwells—and God dwells among us.

In Scripture Zion is not only a physical place, as I've already pointed out. It is a people as well. God described His people as Zion. When you look for Zion, you are looking for a people. You're looking for a certain group of people who live in Zion, whose reality and identity are established in the realm of God.

A CLEARER VISION OF THE HEAVENLY ZION

To get a greater understanding of what Zion is, let's go to Hebrews 12 and let me give you a new covenant scripture that connects what I'm saying here. In verse 22 the writer tells the believers, "But you have come to Mount Zion and to the city of the living God, the heavenly Jerusalem" (NKJV). Notice that he was writing to Hebrews. These are people, Hebrews, Jews, who all their lives were connected to earthly Zion, Jerusalem, the city, the temple, the priesthood, the feasts, Passover, Pentecost, and Tabernacles. This was the same beautiful temple the disciples told Jesus they admired, and the Lord responded by telling them it would be destroyed (Matt. 24:1–3; Mark 13:1–2; Luke 21:5–7).

But now the writer to the Hebrews is telling them, you are no longer connected to the earthly. You're now connected to the heavenly. You've come to something greater than what you have been used to. You've come to the reality of which the city was just a type and a picture.

Yes, we still have a city named Jerusalem on the earth even now. I have visited it, and it was a great experience. But my reality goes beyond even that. My reality is heavenly. I have something greater than the earthly. We all do.

Being Heaven on Earth

Look what it says in Hebrews 12:22–23, "You have come to Mount Zion and to the city of the living God, the heavenly Jerusalem, and into an innumerable company of angels, to the general assembly and church of the firstborn" (NKJV).

It's saying here that you come to the church. The church is the heavenly Jerusalem, Mount Zion, the city of God. Did you realize—and this is amazing—that even though you're on earth, you are of a heavenly people? You are in this world but not of it because your citizenship is in heaven.

The hardest part about living for God is how to be heavenly on earth. It's not easy because when you're heavenly, people can say that you are too deep or too spiritual. The challenge is how to be heavenly and still pay your bills, how to be heavenly and still brush your teeth, how to be heavenly and still enjoy life, and how to be a heavenly people living on the earth. Those are the difficult parts because we're so used to being earthly. But then you get baptized in the Holy Ghost and start having dreams, having visions, prophesying, and praying; you get the anointing. You get an unction. The Word of God comes alive to you, and then you start, if you're not careful, being spooky. This is the difficult part—how to be heavenly without being spooky, without floating into rooms, looking at everybody. But this is what it is to be heavenly while still living on earth.

Is Your Church a Zion Church?

Though we are discovering we are Zion, we should also find places to worship that are what I call Zion churches. Zion churches keep the reality of Zion alive within us. Zion churches make the glory and presence of God their pursuit. The presence of God is welcome in their midst. Zion churches expect to tap into the miracle realm. They expect to activate the prophetic in every service. They expect to make a joyful noise to the Lord and to worship until the glory of God comes.

You may be thinking, "Brother Eckhardt, how do I know if I'm in a Zion church? Is it a church named Zion, Mount Zion, Greater Zion, New Zion, Holy Zion, or Big Zion?"

Go back to Psalm 132, and let's look at verse 16. It says, "I will also clothe her priests with salvation, and her saints shall shout aloud for joy." So I'll ask you, "Is there any shouting in that church?"

"Shouting?" you may be thinking. "You mean shouting is a sign of Zion?"

Yes, it is. "Let them shout aloud for joy," the Bible says. In other words, Zion is such a place of God's presence that her priests and kings are clothed with salvation and deliverance, and they shout aloud for joy.

"Well, I don't want to go to a shouting church."

You don't want Zion.

"I want to go to a quiet church where everybody just worships nice and quiet. Maybe a little hallelujah or amen every now and then, but not too loud. All that 'Lift your voice and shout glory!'—I don't want that."

Well again, and I hate to tell you this, but you must not want Zion, because shouting is a sign of victory.

Lance Wallnau has written, "It's a voice-activated universe." He said something I never thought of before. In addressing how the voice breaks barriers in our lives, he said certain things would not be released in your life unless you open your mouth and speak loudly, because your voice is connected to your spirit.[6] That's why the Bible talks about crying out to God (Ps. 18:6; 77:1; 120:1; 141:1). Some things don't happen unless you cry out, lift your voice, and shout. It's something spiritual. You can't just be quiet all the time.

There are times, of course, for quietness and meditation. Screaming just to be screaming is aggravating and pointless and has no connection to the anointing. There is nothing worse than an unanointed screamer.

Zion is a place of shouting, a place of victory, a place of dancing, a place of celebration, a place of joy, a place of glory, a place of God's presence. It's a place of singing, a place of rejoicing, and a place of worship because the presence of God dwells there. When I look for Zion, I always look for the presence of God. I always look for shouting, dancing, rejoicing, liberty, and glory. I look for singing. I look for the prophetic. I look for victory. I look for the saints of God to be clothed with salvation. I'm not looking for a building or sophisticated people. I'm not looking for people who look religious. I'm listening for a sound.

LISTEN FOR THE SOUND OF ZION

There's a sound in Zion. That sound is the voice of the Lord heard and released from the midst of God's people. Zion is wherever God's people gather, a heavenly people, a people who will worship Him in spirit and in truth. This is where God makes His habitation among those who receive the full revelation of Christ, those who look toward a city with "foundations, whose builder and maker is God" (Heb. 11:10). These are His Zion believers, and when they gather in praise and worship, they're tapping into heaven on earth. We're not here just singing some songs. When we prophesy and shout and feel the glory of God's anointing come in, that's heaven. That's heaven right here.

Some people don't realize what is available to them. They may say, "The world is just so full of hell. It's just so bad. It's just terrible. There are killings and murders." But you can have heaven on earth. You can live in that realm where you touch the heavenly because you live with a continual awareness you are in Christ, positioned in God. When you go to a Zion church, you're used to the heavenly. You're used to the sounds and songs of heaven, the glory of heaven, the presence of heaven, the power and anointing of heaven, the reign of heaven, and the blessings of heaven. You're used to that. You touch heaven. Even though you live on the earth, you're always touching heaven because you are of a heavenly people.

God did not call us to be earthly religious people merely performing some religious ritual, "Om! Om!"

I was in Uganda in the 1990s. I was in my hotel sleeping when suddenly loudspeakers blared an Arabic message. I woke up startled, wondering, "What in the world?" It was five o'clock in the morning! I called the front desk and said, "What is going on here? I didn't come here to be jolted awake like this at five o'clock in the morning. What's going on?"

"Well," they said, "we have some Muslim guests here, and we gave them permission to pray."

I admit that I was vexed by this Muslim prayer call that blasted into my hotel room at five o'clock in the morning when I was trying to sleep. That was not a pleasing sound. It's religious and carries no presence. But when you get around Zion, there's a sound that activates the power of God with new songs and prophecy. That is the atmosphere of Zion, and God has desired to dwell there forever.

From generation to generation there will always be a Zion. There will always be a people. There will always be a group who knows the joyful sound because they know how to praise and worship and invite God's presence in. There'll always be a group of people who are not concerned about form and fashion, but they love God. They love His presence and glory. They settle for nothing less than Zion because they know that's where the blessing is.

God says, "I will abundantly bless her provision."

I don't know about you, but I will always be in Zion. You'll never catch me in a dead church—never. I'll drive right by it and go to McDonald's instead! I'll pull up and order a number two. No, you will not find me in a dead, dry-bone church with no glory, no presence. That's two hours of life I'll never get back. I'm looking for Zion. No matter where I go, I will find it. I'll search and search: "I know somewhere in this city there's a Zion. It may not be the biggest church, it may not have the best building, but I will find the people who know God's glory and how to shout, praise, bless God, and rejoice. I will find those people."

I'm not looking for their color. They can be black, white, green, red, or blue. I don't care. I'm not looking at the color or a name. I'm listening for a sound and looking for an anointing. I'm looking for power and glory. It doesn't matter how they look or what the name is on the building. I belong in Zion. I belong in the place of glory. I refuse to worship false priests, idols, and kingdoms that men set up.

I've experienced heaven on earth. I have experienced glory. I know what it is like to be in the presence of God. I know shalom, peace, and joy. I know righteousness and what it feels like. I know what it is to worship in a Zion church. I'm used to it, and that's where you will find me. Now, you can go over to Dry Church, Tumbleweed Christian Center, Jurassic Park Assembly, or Bone Dry Christian Center. Go ahead. Not me. I don't have time for it. You will find me in Zion, where God has made His habitation. How about you?

PRAYER OF THANKSGIVING FOR ZION

Lord, I thank You for Zion. It is Your dwelling place. It's where You rest forever. It's a place of shouting, a place of joy, and a place of Your glory. I will always live and abide in Zion. Thank You, Lord, for calling me to Zion.

Chapter 3

BORN OF ZION

But Jerusalem which is above is free, which is the mother of us all.
—Galatians 4:26

As we are born again in Christ, we become the children of the heavenly Zion. We are born into the freedom of the new covenant because the heavenly Jerusalem is our mother. Pastor Hedley Palmer says it like this when he discusses Psalm 87:4:

> God says, "I will make mention of Rahab (used for Egypt) and Babylon to them that know me, behold Philistia and Tyre, with Ethiopia, this man was born there." To be born in the places mentioned was no honour to God. But most of us delight in the place where we were born. What really counts with God is the place where you were born again. Every city on earth is a "mean" city compared with the city of God. "And of Zion it shall be said, this and that man was born there." Here is a lovely Hebraism—"this and that man was born there" = a man a man was born there. This is an expression only Hebrews use. The idea behind the phrase is a man who was really a man was born there. Born in Egypt? Born in Babylon? Born in Tyre? So what? but of Zion it was said, a man was born there. Those born there were God's men. My greatest joy is to be able to say I was born again in Mount Zion—City of our God.[1]

In the Book of Isaiah we read, "Who hath heard such a thing? who hath seen such things? Shall the earth be made to bring forth in one day? or shall a nation be born at once? for as soon as Zion travailed, she brought forth her children" (Isa. 66:8). Zion brought forth her children as soon as she travailed, and a nation was born in a day. The church, too, came forth quickly at Pentecost after the Holy Spirit fell on believers in an upper room, and three thousand were added to their numbers through one sermon. (See Acts 2.) Those who are born of God are the children of Zion. They are new creations in Him and have the characteristics and spiritual DNA of Zion.

I want to make it clear that to receive all the benefits and blessings we have uncovered and will continue to uncover in this book, you must be born again in Zion (John 3). You must be born from above. You must be born of water and Spirit. No other birth compares to the spiritual birth that takes place in Zion. Your natural birth does not give you access to the city of God. Spiritual birth is the only birth that matters in the kingdom.

Again, the psalmist wrote:

> I will make mention of Rahab and Babylon to them that know me: behold Philistia, and Tyre, with Ethiopia; this man was born there. And of Zion it shall be said, This and that man was born in her: and the highest himself shall establish her.
>
> —PSALM 87:4–5

God registers and counts as citizens the people born in Zion—those who are new creations in Christ and have been born of the incorruptible seed of the Word of God (1 Pet. 1:23). The children of Zion have been created by God and are joyful in their King. (See Psalm 149:2.)

The prophet Isaiah wrote that the children of the Lord were "for signs and for wonders in Israel from the LORD of hosts, which dwelleth in mount Zion" (Isa. 8:18). Likewise the children of Zion are for signs and wonders. You are Zion. That means you are a sign. You are a wonder, and your life will speak.

As Zion we also can expect blessing to fall upon our land

because the children of Zion are told to rejoice for the rain, which represents blessings from heaven.

> Be glad then, ye children of Zion, and rejoice in the LORD your God: for he hath given you the former rain moderately, and he will cause to come down for you the rain, the former rain, and the latter rain in the first month.
>
> —JOEL 2:23

> And they shall bring all your brethren for an offering unto the LORD out of all nations upon horses, and in chariots, and in litters, and upon mules, and upon swift beasts, to my holy mountain Jerusalem, saith the LORD, as the children of Israel bring an offering in a clean vessel into the house of the LORD.
>
> —ISAIAH 66:20

WE ARE NEW CREATIONS

The Bible says, "If any man be in Christ, he is a new creature" (2 Cor. 5:17). If you are in Christ, you are a new person, called to serve God in the newness of the Spirit. God is always doing a new thing in Zion (Isa. 42:9; 43:19; 48:6). Zion is filled with new songs and is constantly experiencing new moves of God.

New creatures have new hearts and new spirits (Ezek. 36:26), and as new creatures in Christ we are under a new covenant. Heavenly Zion is the new covenant city. Zion people enjoy the new wine because Zion is the new wineskin. The new wine could not be put in an old wineskin (Matt. 9:17). Yet we enjoy the new wine because we are under the new covenant.

The prophet Joel declared:

> And it shall come to pass in that day, that the mountains shall drop down new wine, and the hills shall flow with milk, and all the rivers of Judah shall flow with waters, and a fountain shall come forth out of the house of the LORD, and shall water the valley of Shittim.
>
> —JOEL 3:18

Wine, milk, rivers, and a fountain are the hallmarks of the kingdom. Zion enjoys this wine, this milk, these rivers, and this fountain. These things flow out of the house of the Lord. Our presses "burst out with new wine" (Prov. 3:10). New wine was always a symbol of blessing, new harvest, prosperity, and joy. You are Zion, and as such, you are a new-wine believer.

CHRIST'S RULE AND REIGN IN ZION

And again, Isaiah says, "The Root of Jesse will spring up, one who will arise to rule over the nations; in him the Gentiles will hope."

—ROMANS 15:12, NIV

The earthly Zion was the city of David, the king of Israel, whom God chose and anointed. Jesus the King is a descendant of David, and as such He is of the root of Jesse because Jesse was David's father.

Isaiah prophesied there would be "a rod out of the stem of Jesse, and a Branch shall grow out of his roots" (Isa. 11:1). Micah later prophesied the Lord would reign over the people in Mount Zion, declaring He would rule over a strong nation.

And I will make her that halted a remnant, and her that was cast far off a strong nation: and the LORD shall reign over them in mount Zion from henceforth, even for ever.

—MICAH 4:7

Those who dwell in Zion submit to the authority of the King because Zion is the place of God's rule and reign. The prophets looked forward to the reign of the Messiah, which would bring salvation, peace, and prosperity to the nations.

The King James Version only uses the word Messiah twice, both times in the Book of Daniel (Dan. 9:25–26).[2] Messiah is the anointed one.[3] Jesus was anointed (smeared with oil), and in Daniel 9:25 He is called "Messiah the prince" (v. 25). The prophet Ezekiel declared that David would be Israel's prince forever (Ezek.

37:25). Yet this is a reference to Jesus, the Messianic David. Jesus is anointed to rule forever, just as David was anointed to rule over Israel.

> The LORD shall reign forever, even thy God, O Zion, unto all generations. Praise ye the LORD.
>
> —PSALM 146:10

Jesus preached the good news of the kingdom, and the disciples were sent to preach the same message. They proclaimed that the kingdom was at hand, which was already evident through the casting out of demons (Matt. 12:28).

Jesus declared the kingdom was at hand, but He also said it would come without observation (Luke 17:20). This is because the kingdom He spoke of was a spiritual kingdom. Many could not see it because it was spiritual, not earthly or carnal. The kingdom was a mystery, hidden even from the religious leaders.

I have heard many definitions of the kingdom, but I define it as the rule and reign of Christ in the heart through the Holy Spirit. Kingdom people walk in the Spirit—they are filled with the Spirit and led by the Spirit. This is what it takes to abide in the kingdom.

When King Jesus came to Zion, the city welcomed Him. A multitude spread their garments in His path while others cut down branches and spread them on the road (Matt. 21:8). As Jesus made His way into Jerusalem, they cried, "Hosanna to the son of David: Blessed is he that cometh in the name of the Lord" (Matt. 21:9).

This was foretold by the prophet Zechariah:

> Tell ye the daughter of Sion, Behold, thy King cometh unto thee, meek, and sitting upon an ass, and a colt the foal of an ass.
>
> —MATTHEW 21:5

The children of Zion recognized the King, and they cried out, "Hosanna." God perfected praise out of the mouth of babes and sucklings (Ps. 8:2). But the Pharisees, who wanted to maintain the old, were displeased and rejected the King. The King came to Zion because it is the city of the King, the place from which He rules. The King sits on the throne in Zion.

Because you are Zion, you are under the rule and reign of Christ. Your life is submitted to the control of the Holy Spirit, which causes you to experience peace (shalom), blessing, favor, and protection.

LIVING UNDER THE PEACE AND PROSPERITY OF GOD

And in mercy shall the throne be established: and he shall sit upon it in truth in the tabernacle of David, judging, and seeking judgment, and hasting righteousness.

—ISAIAH 16:5

The tabernacle of David is synonymous with the kingdom. David's tabernacle is his house and lineage, and God promised David that his seed would sit on his throne (Ps. 132:11). Jesus is the son of David, and He now sits on the throne of David (Acts 2:30).

David was a type of Christ, and his kingdom was a type of Christ's kingdom. Spiritually Zion, the city of David, became the city of God. Solomon is also a type of Christ. Solomon's kingdom was a kingdom of peace (shalom), and those who lived under Solomon's reign lived during a time of peace and prosperity. Likewise those who come into the heavenly Zion come under the reign of Christ's peace and prosperity.

Christ's government of peace was spoken of by the prophet Isaiah:

Of the increase of his government and peace there shall be no end, upon the throne of David, and upon his kingdom, to order it, and to establish it with judgment and with justice from henceforth even for ever. The zeal of the LORD of hosts will perform this.

—ISAIAH 9:7

Isaiah's prophecy connects Christ's government with the throne of David. Christ's government is His rule and His kingdom. Peace (shalom) increases as His government increases. His kingdom includes righteousness (justice), and it advances and increases from generation to generation.

God is committed to seeing Zion expand and increase from generation to generation, and the zeal of the Lord will perform this. You are Zion, and you are increasing and expanding. And as you do, you will have peace (shalom).

LIVING UNDER THE REIGN OF GOD

Psalm 2 is a Messianic psalm that describes the opposition to Christ and His placement on the throne.

> Why do the heathen rage, and the people imagine a vain thing? The kings of the earth set themselves, and the rulers take counsel together, against the LORD, and against his anointed, saying, Let us break their bands asunder, and cast away their cords from us.
>
> —PSALM 2:1–3

This is quoted by the early church in Acts 4:25–27. Herod, Pontius Pilate, the Gentiles, and the people of Israel were gathered together against Christ. They were imagining a vain thing in thinking they could prevent Christ and His kingdom from coming forth.

> He that sitteth in the heavens shall laugh: the LORD shall have them in derision. Then shall he speak unto them in his wrath, and vex them in his sore displeasure.
>
> —PSALM 2:4–5

Wicked men could not stop the Lord's plan, and He would deal with them in His wrath, moving from laughter to anger.

In the end the King was set upon the holy hill of Zion. Psalm 2:6 says, "Yet as for Me, I have anointed and firmly installed My King Upon Zion, My holy mountain" (AMP). *The Message* puts it this way: "Don't you know there's a King in Zion? A coronation banquet is spread for him on the holy summit."

Men could not stop His enthronement. His suffering and death were the plan of God for Him to ascend to the throne.

The psalmist went on to say:

> I will declare the decree: the LORD hath said unto me, Thou art my Son; this day have I begotten thee. Ask of me, and I shall give thee the heathen for thine inheritance, and the uttermost parts of the earth for thy possession. Thou shalt break them with a rod of iron; thou shalt dash them in pieces like a potter's vessel.
> —PSALM 2:7–9

Jesus was begotten on the day of His resurrection. Acts 13:33 says, "God hath fulfilled the same unto us their children, in that he hath raised up Jesus again; as it is also written in the second psalm, Thou art my Son, this day have I begotten thee."

The Father gave Him the nations for His inheritance, and Jesus, the King, now judges those who refuse to submit to Him. He breaks them in pieces like a potter's vessel. This is why we must submit to the Lord.

> Be wise now therefore, O ye kings: be instructed, ye judges of the earth. Serve the LORD with fear, and rejoice with trembling. Kiss the Son, lest he be angry, and ye perish from the way, when his wrath is kindled but a little. Blessed are all they that put their trust in him.
> —PSALM 2:10–12

The psalmist makes it clear that it would be wise to serve the Lord with fear and rejoice with trembling. The judges of the earth are told to kiss the Son. Those who put their trust in the Lord will be blessed.

After this promise Isaiah describes a day of judgment:

Then the moon shall be confounded, and the sun ashamed,
when the Lord of hosts shall reign in mount Zion, and in
Jerusalem, and before his ancients gloriously.

—Isaiah 24:23

At this point, earthly Jerusalem was judged, and Jesus wept
over the city because He saw the desolation that was coming. The
Olivet discourse found in Matthew 24 gave the details of the judgment that was coming.

Isaiah said the Lord of hosts would reign in Zion, and God
would establish His rule through judgment. God would judge
the rebellion and apostasy of the nation and establish Zion in
righteousness.

This is what Jesus came to do. He came to establish the kingdom
of God. He came to establish righteousness and to rule and reign
over His people. You are that people because you are Zion. You
have been established by Christ and are the righteousness of God
in Christ.

In John's revelation he wrote of hearing "the voice of a great
multitude, and as the voice of many waters, and as the voice of
mighty thunderings, saying, Alleluia: for the Lord God omnipotent reigneth" (Rev. 19:6). We are the ones who cry hallelujah, the
Lord God omnipotent reigns. *Hallelujah* means praise Yah (Jah).
Jesus is Jah, as Psalm 68:4 says: "Sing unto God, sing praises to
his name: extol him that rideth upon the heavens by his name Jah,
and rejoice before him." We praise Him in Zion because He reigns.

There is no better place to live than under the reign of God.
We are the habitation of God, and we reside under His safety and
protection in a land free of wild beasts (Ezek. 34:25). We are the
strong city of Zion, and we dwell in a place of rest.

Psalm 72, written by Solomon, is both a picture of his reign and
a prophecy concerning Christ and His kingdom. The King "shall
come down like rain upon the mown grass: as showers that water
the earth. In his days shall the righteous flourish; and abundance

of peace so long as the moon endureth....Yea, all kings shall fall down before him: all nations shall serve him. For he shall deliver the needy when he crieth; the poor also, and him that hath no helper....And blessed be his glorious name for ever: and let the whole earth be filled with his glory; Amen, and Amen" (vv. 6–7, 11–12, 19).

This is a picture of the King who reigns in Zion. Is it any wonder the multitude cries, "Alleluia: for the Lord God omnipotent reigneth"?

LIVING UNDER THE JUSTICE OF GOD

> But unto the Son he saith, Thy throne, O God, is for ever and
> ever: a sceptre of righteousness is the sceptre of thy kingdom.
> —HEBREWS 1:8

A scepter is an ornamental staff carried by rulers as a symbol of sovereignty.[4] The Son's scepter is righteousness (justice). Zion is a place of the scepter, a place of righteousness and justice. Psalm 89:14 says justice is the habitation of God's throne. There is no righteousness apart from justice.

God is just, and His kingdom is a kingdom of justice. To live under the rule of God is to live under the justice of God. Jeremiah 31:23 says, "The LORD bless thee, O habitation of justice, and mountain of holiness." Notice that the mountain of holiness is also the habitation of justice. Zion believers believe in justice and hate injustice. You are Zion, and that means you are just.

People will not hurt or destroy on the holy mountain (Isa. 65:25). In other words, there is no injustice on the holy mountain. The unjust cannot dwell in Zion (Rev. 22:11). Justice is what people desire, and it can be found in Zion: the place of fairness and righteousness. With so much injustice in the world, we need Zion. We need a righteous and just ruler. Jesus is that righteous ruler. Jeremiah 23:5 says, "Behold, the days come, saith the LORD, that

I will raise unto David a righteous Branch, and a King shall reign and prosper, and shall execute judgment and justice in the earth."

Jesus reigns in Zion. Jesus rules and reigns over His people in justice and righteousness. His rule is fair and equitable, so you can trust His dominion. What an honor to live in Zion, where we never need to fear injustice. What an honor to be Zion and live under the rule of the King.

> The Lord reigneth, he is clothed with majesty; the Lord is clothed with strength, wherewith he hath girded himself: the world also is stablished, that it cannot be moved.
>
> —Psalm 93:1

Called by God's Name

God chose to place His name in Jerusalem (Zion). Zion is the place of God, and His name is known there. We do not have the names of the false gods in our lips (Ps. 16:4). Zion believers are called by God's name, and we glorify His name in Zion (2 Thess. 1:12). We are His, and He has given us His name to wield and to wear.

We come to Zion seeking His habitation.

> But unto the place which the Lord your God shall choose out of all your tribes to put his name there, even unto his habitation shall ye seek, and thither thou shalt come.
>
> —Deuteronomy 12:5

God's name is in His habitation. We gather in the name of Jesus (Matt. 18:20). We call upon the name of the Lord Jesus Christ (1 Cor. 1:2). We cast out devils in His name (Mark 16:17). The name of Jesus is above every name (Phil. 2:9).

The names of God reveal His character. God's name is great in Zion. We praise His "great and terrible name" (Ps. 99:3). God promised to sanctify His name, which had been blasphemed through Israel's disobedience (Ezek. 36:23). From the rising of the sun to the going down of the same, God's name would be great among the nations (Mal. 1:11). God's "name is dreadful among the heathen" (Mal. 1:14).

We give unto the LORD the glory due His name (Ps. 29:2). The name of the Lord is declared in Zion (Ps. 102:21). We give thanks unto His name (Ps. 122:4). We exalt the name of the Lord (Ps. 34:3). We rejoice in his name (Ps. 89:16).

I love to sing about the names of God. We sing about El Shaddai, El Elyon, Yahweh, Jehovah Jireh, Jehovah Rapha, Jehovah Nissi, Jehovah Shalom, Jehovah Shammah, almighty God, the mighty God, everlasting Father, Prince of Peace, Wonderful, Lord of hosts, Counselor, the Most High, I Am, Word of God, Alpha and Omega, Holy One, and Lion of the tribe of Judah.

God reveals Himself to us through His name. His name reveals His character, nature, and power. God's name is known and heard in Zion. Zion believers and Zion churches love the name of God.

We bring our offerings to Zion. Giving is a major part of the lifestyle of the Zion believer. It is one way we honor the Lord. Zion believers are givers. You are Zion. You are a giver.

> Then there shall be a place which the LORD your God shall choose to cause his name to dwell there; thither shall ye bring all that I command you; your burnt offerings, and your sacrifices, your tithes, and the heave offering of your hand, and all your choice vows which ye vow unto the LORD.
>
> —DEUTERONOMY 12:11

Strong nations come to Him and bring offerings. The nations bring their forces (*chayil*) to Zion. We bring offerings and come into His courts (Ps. 96:8).

> In that time shall the present be brought unto the LORD of hosts of a people scattered and peeled, and from a people terrible from their beginning hitherto; a nation meted out and trodden under foot, whose land the rivers have spoiled, to the place of the name of the LORD of hosts, the mount Zion.
>
> —ISAIAH 18:7

Psalm 76:11 says, "Vow, and pay unto the LORD your God: let all that be round about him bring presents unto him that ought to be feared." The Easy-to-Read Version says, "People everywhere fear and respect God, and they will bring gifts to him." Psalm 68:29 says, "Because of thy temple at Jerusalem shall kings bring presents unto thee." God remembers our offerings (Ps. 20:3). Offerings are brought to the holy mountain (Isa. 66:20).

WELCOME TO THE TABLE OF THE LORD

Zion is a place of feasting. A feast is a banquet. We feast before the Lord. "He that is of a merry heart hath a continual feast" (Prov. 15:15). Isaiah 25:6 says, "And in this mountain shall the LORD of hosts make unto all people a feast of fat things, a feast of wines on the lees, of fat things full of marrow, of wines on the lees well refined."

> If the place which the LORD thy God hath chosen to put his name there be too far from thee, then thou shalt kill of thy herd and of thy flock, which the LORD hath given thee, as I have commanded thee, and thou shalt eat in thy gates whatsoever thy soul lusteth after.
> —DEUTERONOMY 12:21

We eat and worship before the Lord in Zion. Psalm 22:29 says, "All they that be fat upon earth shall eat and worship: all they that go down to the dust shall bow before him: and none can keep alive his own soul." Israel was commanded to eat and rejoice before the Lord (Deut. 12:7, 18). They were to eat in the place where the Lord chose to put His name. They were to eat before the Lord year by year (Deut. 15:20).

> And thou shalt eat before the LORD thy God, in the place which he shall choose to place his name there, the tithe of thy corn, of thy wine, and of thine oil, and the firstlings of

thy herds and of thy flocks; that thou mayest learn to fear
the Lord thy God always.

—Deuteronomy 14:23

The name of the Lord is declared in Zion. His name brings
healing and deliverance. Whatever we ask in that name is granted
to us (John 15:16). We receive from God in that name, and our joy
is full (John 16:24).

...to declare the name of the Lord in Zion, and his praise
in Jerusalem.

—Psalm 102:21

Zion is the place where people call upon the name of the Lord.
Those who call upon His name are saved and delivered. There is
no salvation apart from the name of Jesus. There is no other name
given under heaven whereby we can be saved (Acts 4:12).

And it shall come to pass, that whosoever shall call on the
name of the Lord shall be delivered: for in mount Zion and
in Jerusalem shall be deliverance, as the Lord hath said, and
in the remnant whom the Lord shall call.

—Joel 2:32

THE LORD SINGS OVER YOU

We have heard teaching on enjoying God, but did you know God
enjoys us?

The Lord hath taken away thy judgments, he hath cast out
thine enemy: the king of Israel, even the Lord, is in the
midst of thee: thou shalt not see evil any more. In that day
it shall be said to Jerusalem, Fear thou not: and to Zion, Let
not thine hands be slack. The Lord thy God in the midst
of thee is mighty; he will save, he will rejoice over thee with
joy; he will rest in his love, he will joy over thee with singing.

—Zephaniah 3:15–17

Zion is free. Evil cannot rule over Zion. The Lord has cast out the enemy. The Lord in our midst is mighty. Don't be afraid. Don't let your hands be slack. This is the word of the Lord over Zion.

"The Lord thy God in the midst of thee is mighty" (Zeph. 3:17) is said twice. He will save and deliver you by His might. He will rejoice over you with singing.

I love it when the Lord sings over us. I call this the song from the Lord. There is a song to the Lord and a song from the Lord. God enjoys His people. God takes pleasure in His people (Ps. 149:4). God is not angry with you; God rejoices over you.

You are Zion, the place of God's delight. Zion is God's joy—you are God's joy. Allow this reality to shape your identity. God delights in *you*.

God enjoys His people. God shouts over us. You are Zion. God rejoices over you.

God rejoices over Zion as a groom rejoices over his bride. You were created to bring God pleasure and joy. Zion is like a bride adorned for her husband (Rev. 21:2).

> For as a young man marrieth a virgin, so shall thy sons marry thee: and as the bridegroom rejoiceth over the bride, so shall thy God rejoice over thee.
>
> —Isaiah 62:5

The marriage motif is connected to God remarrying Israel. This is a picture of the new covenant. God had promised to betroth Israel in righteousness and faithfulness (Isa. 54:5; Hos. 2:19–20). God now has a new covenant with His people. This new covenant included the Gentiles.

Liberty and Grace Is Yours

The Book of Hebrews emphasizes the superiority of the new covenant over the old covenant. Jesus is greater than Moses. Melchizedek is greater than Levi. Grace is greater than the Law.

Hebrews also compares two mountains. Mount Zion (the new) is greater than Mount Sinai (the old).

> For ye are not come unto the mount that might be touched, and that burned with fire, nor unto blackness, and darkness, and tempest....But ye are come unto mount Sion, and unto the city of the living God, the heavenly Jerusalem, and to an innumerable company of angels, to the general assembly and church of the firstborn, which are written in heaven, and to God the Judge of all, and to the spirits of just men made perfect.
> —HEBREWS 12:18, 22–23

Mount Sinai represents the law with its judgments. Mount Sinai is called Hagar (Gal. 4:25). Hagar was a slave woman. Jerusalem had become Hagar (v. 25), who represents bondage. The law had become a yoke. Isaac was the son of the free woman. Isaac was the child of promise. Isaac represents freedom and liberty.

The Hebrew believers were leaving the old and coming into the new. They were coming to Mount Zion, the heavenly Jerusalem, the church of the firstborn. They were leaving bondage and coming into freedom. Zion and her children were now breaking forth (Gal. 4:27). Zion's children are born free. Zion's children are born of the Spirit and not of the flesh.

The old covenant was waxing old and vanishing away (Heb. 8:13). The kingdom of God was arriving (Heb. 12:28). The nations were entering into the kingdom. The old covenant was fighting the new. Some of Christ's followers were returning to the old because of persecution. Hebrews is a warning not to go back. Freedom is our Zion.

PLANTED IN THE MOUNTAIN OF GOD

> Thou shalt bring them in, and plant them in the mountain of thine inheritance, in the place, O LORD, which thou hast made for thee to dwell in, in the Sanctuary, O LORD, which

thy hands have established. The LORD shall reign for ever and ever.

—EXODUS 15:17–18

Zion was also the mountain of God, God's holy hill. It was always the purpose of God to bring His people to this mountain, His sanctuary. The sanctuary was the place of His power and glory. The Exodus passage is also the first time in Scripture that the eternal reign of God is mentioned. This connects the mountain to the kingdom, the place of God's rule and reign.

A mountain is a picture of a kingdom. It is a picture of power and strength. Jesus smites the kingdoms and becomes a great mountain (Dan. 2:35). Zion is a great mountain. Zion is the place of power and dominion.

Mount Zion cannot be removed. The kingdom of God is an immovable kingdom (Heb. 12:28). Zion remains steadfast and strong from generation to generation. Kingdoms rise and fall, but God's kingdom is forever.

David said that God had made his mountain to stand strong (Ps. 30:7). He attributed this to God's favor and grace. His mountain was also a symbol of prosperity. God will make your mountain stand strong. You are Zion, the place where God dwells.

> Even them will I bring to my holy mountain, and make them joyful in my house of prayer: their burnt offerings and their sacrifices shall be accepted upon mine altar; for mine house shall be called an house of prayer for all people.
>
> —ISAIAH 56:7

God also brings us to Zion. He makes us joyful in His house of prayer. Joyful prayer is another aspect of Zion. You are Zion. You are a house of prayer. Zion churches are praying churches, and Zion believers are praying believers.

The prayers of David ended after he prayed for the whole earth to be filled with God's glory (Ps. 72:19–20). Zion prays for God's glory to cover the earth. Habakkuk prophesied that "the earth shall be filled with the knowledge of the glory of the LORD, as the waters cover the sea" (Hab. 2:14).

Zion consists of all people and nations. Zion has no geographical or ethnic boundaries. The wall of partition between Jew and Gentile has been broken down. All the nations come to Zion, the mountain of God.

> And it shall come to pass in the last days, that the mountain of the LORD's house shall be established in the top of the mountains, and shall be exalted above the hills; and all nations shall flow unto it.
>
> —ISAIAH 2:2

This mountain was established in the last days. The mountain of the Lord's house was established in the top of the mountains. All nations come to pray, worship, and sacrifice. You are Zion. You pray, worship, and sacrifice in the highest mountain, the kingdom of God. This mountain is exalted above all mountains.

Zion is the highest place. *Mountain* means the head—that which stands above the rest.[5] Being in Christ is the highest position. This is your identity in Christ. This is who you are. This is the place of promotion and exaltation. You do not live in a low place. You are Zion.

We ascend to Zion. Those with pure hearts and clean hands ascend (Ps. 24:3–5). We receive the blessing of the Lord. Zion is God's holy mountain. Zion people are holy people. In ancient times the Hebrews would sing the Psalms of Ascent as they were going up to the physical Zion.

> They shall ask the way to Zion with their faces thitherward, saying, Come, and let us join ourselves to the LORD in a perpetual covenant that shall not be forgotten.
>
> —JEREMIAH 50:5

People are looking for the way to heavenly Zion and to join themselves to the Lord in a covenant. They are searching and inquiring. People are looking for the place of glory, blessing, favor, power, and God's presence.

People come to Zion to learn the ways of God and how to walk in His paths (Mic. 4:2). They come to learn the Word of God. Zion is a place of teaching and instruction. Zion believers love the Word of God. Zion loves teaching and instruction and knowledge.

People will come to you to learn the ways of God. They will come to you for instruction. You are Zion. You have the Word of the Lord. Jesus, the teacher, lives in you.

Zion has the knowledge of the glory. The glory realm is known in Zion. This is the realm of majesty, brilliance, splendor, and light. Nations will come to you because of His light, and kings will come to you because of the brightness of His glory upon you (Isa. 60:3). I will deal extensively with this realm in this book and discuss in-depth the glory of Zion.

Chapter 4

THE RIVER OF GOD

*There is a river, the streams whereof shall make glad the city
of God, the holy place of the tabernacles of the most High.*
—Psalm 46:4

As part of discovering the revelation of Zion, another of my favorite subjects in the Scriptures is the river of God. Cities are usually built near rivers and large bodies of water. This is because people need water to sustain life. Zion has a river that brings and sustains life. It is a source of life. God's river is a picture and type of the Holy Spirit, which brings new life into the hearts and souls of every believer. And just as the Holy Spirit flows in our lives, He also flows among our assemblies when we gather to worship.

The river that runs through the holy city of God is a symbol of the Spirit of God flowing through the heart of each believer where He takes up residence. Since we are discovering ourselves to be Zion, the very seat of the Spirit of God, we can understand that the river of God flows through us.

In Ezekiel 47 and Revelation 22, prophets Ezekiel and John, respectively, both saw the river in a vision. John saw the river flowing from the throne. This connects the river to the kingdom. There is a river in Zion.

Jesus speaks of the rivers of living water that flow from the believer. This river is a source of life and refreshing. There is a river of healing, a river of miracles. There is a river of deliverance, a river of prophecy, and a river of praise and worship.

He that believeth on me, as the scripture hath said, out of his
belly shall flow rivers of living water.

—John 7:38

The belly is the innermost being, the spirit. This is a spiritual
river. The river brings blessing and produces life wherever it goes
(Ezek. 47:9). Zion churches are river churches. You are Zion. The
Holy Spirit flows from you as you speak, pray, and minister.

Zechariah prophesied that living water would flow from
Jerusalem (Zion). Zion releases living water to the nations. This
water brings healing.

And it shall be in that day, that living waters shall go out
from Jerusalem; half of them toward the former sea, and
half of them toward the hinder sea: in summer and in winter
shall it be.

—Zechariah 14:8

Jerusalem can be a picture of the heart, the spirit, the belly. As
pastor and Bible researcher Todd Dennis says, "The entirety of the
Bible abounds with references of Jerusalem that are clearly—for
those willing to see—to be taken in a personal sense regarding the
presence of the Lord and kingdom growth within His people."[1]

The streams make glad the city of God. You are the city of God.
Gladness comes to you from this river. We serve the Lord with
gladness (Ps. 100:2). The daughters are glad in Zion (Ps. 48:11).

Does the river flow in your life? Does prophecy flow in your life?
Is there a flow of new songs from your mouth? Do the gifts of the
Spirit flow from your life? This should be normal if you are Zion.

HEALING AND RESTORATION

And it shall come to pass, that every thing that liveth, which
moveth, whithersoever the rivers shall come, shall live: and
there shall be a very great multitude of fish, because these

waters shall come thither: for they shall be healed; and every thing shall live whither the river cometh.

—Ezekiel 47:9

The river of God brings healing and restoration. Everything the river touches lives. This river waters dry places, satisfies the parched ground, and brings life to the desert.

Ezekiel was taken into a river. The river went beyond his ankles, knees, and loins (waist), and above his shoulders. It was a river to swim in (Ezek. 47:1–6). Ezekiel saw all manner of trees for meat on the banks of this river. We eat from these trees in Zion. These trees produce health and strength. The fruit is for meat (which gives strength), and the leaves are for medicine (Ezek. 47:12).

INTO THE DEEP

Ezekiel's river is a picture of the river of life that flows from the temple. It is a spiritual river that has different depths. We can go to depths in the Spirit and the Word, represented by water that is ankle-deep, knee-deep, loins-deep, shoulder- or neck-deep, or over our heads. The depths are measured by one thousand cubits. One thousand is a perfect number that represents the kingdom of God. One thousand represents increase, multiplication, and abundance. God desires to increase in us revelation, wisdom, power, grace, favor, and authority. There is no limit to the depths of God and the Spirit. There are different levels (shallow, middle, and deep).

The water comes to the ankles (shallow).

> Direct contact with the power of the Holy Spirit is absolutely wonderful, but do not forget that "ankle-deep" is God's minimum![2]

> And when the man that had the line in his hand went forth eastward, he measured a thousand cubits, and he brought me through the waters; the waters were to the ankles.
>
> —Ezekiel 47:3

The water comes to the knees and the loins or middle. The middle is halfway. Some believers go halfway and stop.

> Again he measured a thousand, and brought me through the waters; the waters were to the knees. Again he measured a thousand, and brought me through; the waters were to the loins.
>
> —Ezekiel 47:4

The water comes above the shoulders and head (deep). When water goes over the head, you must be able to swim. You must swim in the deep. The Scriptures have much to say about the deep. The deep is a place of wonders:

> These see the works of the Lord, and his wonders in the deep.
>
> —Psalm 107:24

The deep is a place of abundance:

> Now when he had left speaking, he said unto Simon, Launch out into the deep, and let down your nets for a draught.
>
> —Luke 5:4

The deep is a place of praise:

> Praise the Lord from the earth, ye dragons, and all deeps.
>
> —Psalm 148:7

The deep is a place of wisdom:

> The words of a man's mouth are as deep waters, and the wellspring of wisdom as a flowing brook.
>
> —Proverbs 18:4

The deep is a place of counsel:

> Counsel in the heart of man is like deep water; but a man of understanding will draw it out.
>
> —Proverbs 20:5

The deep is a place of revelation:

But God hath revealed them unto us by his Spirit: for the Spirit searcheth all things, yea, the deep things of God.

—1 Corinthians 2:10

The deep is a place of apostolic suffering:

Thrice was I beaten with rods, once was I stoned, thrice I suffered shipwreck, a night and a day I have been in the deep.

—2 Corinthians 11:25

The deep has a voice:

The mountains saw thee, and they trembled: the overflowing of the water passed by: the deep uttered his voice, and lifted up his hands on high.

—Habakkuk 3:10

There are blessings in the deep:

Even by the God of thy father, who shall help thee; and by the Almighty, who shall bless thee with blessings of heaven above, blessings of the deep that lieth under, blessings of the breasts, and of the womb.

—Genesis 49:25

Zion believers go deeper. The worship is deeper. The revelation is deeper. The prophetic is deeper. The wisdom is deeper. You are Zion. You are deep. The river of God flows in your life. Don't be afraid to launch out and go deeper. Here is a prophetic word concerning the deep:

Out in the ocean you will go. You will leave the shores behind. You will go into the deep, and new things you will find. You will leave that familiar place, and you will go out by My grace. No longer will you be held back, but I'm giving you wealth. No more lack. You will go out into the deep, and new treasures you will find. You will go out into the new, and the old you will leave behind. No longer will you be afraid, but you will boldly go. You will go beyond the waves, and the deep things you will know, for I've come to take you there, into a place you have never been to. I come that you might launch out.

Yes, in a new place I will send you out. You will no longer see the land, but you'll go out beyond the waves, and I will take you by the hands, and you will go out into the deep, into a far, distant place. You will know My grace and treasures. You will know the abundance of My grace. My wind is blowing you away from a familiar place, a place you have always known. I'm taking you away from that place. Do not be afraid, My children. Do not be afraid to go. I'm going to send you out into the deep, and new things you will know. You will see things you've never seen before and go places you've never gone to before. You will do things you've never done before. You will receive more and more, for I've been waiting on you to say yes to Me and lay aside all the fear to leave the land behind, to get away from that which is near, to go wide and far beyond anyplace you've gone before. Oh yes, I'm opening for you. I'm opening up a brand-new door, so don't be afraid, but step into this place where I'm taking you. Yes, I'm taking you out of the old into the new. Allow My wind to blow, and allow the season to change, and to the new place you will go. For truly the wind has come and is blowing now, and you will enjoy the new place I'm taking you to, and you will say, "My God! Wow! I never knew I could go out this far, far beyond the shore. I never knew how great it could be until the wind took me there."

Zion is a place of health and healing. It is not a dry place; it is well-watered. Zion is lush and flourishing like Eden, the garden of the Lord. You are Zion. You are the garden of the Lord.

> For the Lord shall comfort Zion: he will comfort all her waste places; and he will make her wilderness like Eden, and her desert like the garden of the Lord; joy and gladness shall be found therein, thanksgiving, and the voice of melody.
> —Isaiah 51:3

You are watered, and you water others. You release life wherever you go. Your words are containers of life to pour out upon the thirsty. Zion churches release the river of God to flood the dry places and to cause deserts and waste places to bloom again. We are enriched with the river of God (Ps. 65:9).

> In the midst of the street of it, and on either side of the river, was there the tree of life, which bare twelve manner of fruits, and yielded her fruit every month: and the leaves of the tree were for the healing of the nations.
>
> —Revelation 22:2

The river of God brings healing to the nations. John's vision culminates with the arrival of the heavenly Jerusalem. Heavenly Zion is the reality of the earthly Zion. Heavenly Zion is new covenant Zion.

Prophetic Flow and the River of God

The tree of life is beside the river. Wisdom is a tree of life (Prov. 3:18). A wholesome tongue is a tree of life (Prov. 15:4). I believe the river of God that flows from the believer is released through words. This river is related through tongues, preaching, teaching, prophecy, and singing.

The sons and daughters prophesy in Zion. The servants and handmaidens prophesy in Zion. The singers and musicians prophesy. We can all prophesy (1 Cor. 14:24, 31). Prophecy is the utterance of the Holy Spirit.

The prophets and the prophetic flow reached their zenith during the days of David and the establishment of Zion. There were the prophets and seers from the families of Asaph, Heman, and Jeduthun (1 Chron. 25). There was Chenaniah, the master of the song [Hebrew word *massa*, meaning burden or prophecy (1 Chron. 15:27)].[3] There was Zadok the seer (2 Sam. 15:27). There were the prophets Gad and Nathan, who, along with David, established Israel's worship (2 Chron. 29:25).

David is called "the sweet psalmist of Israel" (2 Sam. 23:1). The Word of the Lord was in his tongue. David opened dark sayings upon the harp (Ps. 78:2). Zion is a place for psalmists. You are Zion. Let the psalmist be awakened in you (Eph. 5:19).

New songs are sung in Zion (Ps. 33:3; 40:3; 96:1; 98:1; 144:9; 149:1; Isa. 42:10). The song of the Lord is always fresh and new. You are Zion. Sing the new song. Let these songs flow from your belly like a river. These new songs release new things into our lives—the life and blessings of Zion are in that river flow.

God sings over us in Zion. I have seen people healed and delivered when God sings over them. These songs are prophetic and bring edification, exhortation, and comfort (1 Cor. 14:3). We hear and receive the substance of God's own heart through these songs. Wisdom and revelation knowledge rise up within us to release strength when we sing new songs given prophetically from the Lord.

I love activating believers in the prophetic song. All believers can do this. Stir up the gift of God. You are Zion. You can sing over people and release miracles into their lives. Every worship leader should do this. Every psalmist and praise team should do this. You are Zion.

Jesus dwells in Zion. Jesus sings in Zion. Jesus sings through us. This is done through the Holy Spirit, the Spirit of Christ.

> I will declare thy name unto my brethren: in the midst of the congregation will I praise thee.
>
> —PSALM 22:22

> I will declare thy name unto my brethren, in the midst of the church will I sing praise unto thee.
>
> —HEBREWS 2:12

Jesus sings in our midst and in the midst of the church. Jesus was speaking through David prophetically. This prophecy is fulfilled through us.

When you yield to the Holy Spirit in worship, you are yielding to Jesus. Jesus speaks through our mouths. The voice of Jesus is heard in Zion. What a powerful manifestation of the Spirit of Christ. This is Zion. You are Zion. Allow Christ to speak and sing through you.

The Spirit of Christ was speaking through David when he wrote most of the psalms by inspiration. Much of what he spoke through the psalms was actually Christ speaking through him. We can experience the same thing today when we sing psalms by the Holy Spirit. You are Zion, and Christ dwells in you. Allow Him to testify of His goodness and great plan through you as you sing a new song from the Lord.

We must worship in spirit and in truth. True worship cannot happen apart from the Holy Spirit. The baptism of the Holy Spirit enables us to be true worshippers. Zion is the place of true worship, and Zion believers are worshippers. Zion churches are worshipping churches. You are Zion. You are a worshipper.

THE SPRINGS OF ZION

A spring is a fountain, a well, a source.[4] In Psalm 87:7 it says, "All my springs are in thee." This is an interesting verse. I read it many times, and I had to ask, "What does that mean, God? 'All my springs are in thee.'" All my springs are in Zion. It's not talking about springs under your shoes where you jump. Instead this verse is talking about the source of all your blessings being in Zion. Your springs—the source, the fountain, the river—where you draw your blessing from are in Zion. One translation says, "The source of my life springs from Jerusalem!" (NLT). Another says, "All good things come from Jerusalem" (NCV). And another says, "Zion is the source of all our blessings" (GW).

Zion is a place of springs, fountains, and the river of God. It's a place where water flows. It's a place of refreshing, blessing, and life. It is not a dry place. It is a place where good things flow.

I love Zion because the source of every good and perfect expression of God's blessing springs forth from Zion. It's where the blessing is, and so although people may leave Zion and go else-where, Zion remains the place—the source—where refreshing waters, blessings, healing, deliverance, miracles, and breakthrough flow.

STAY OUT OF THE SWAMP

I always tell the story of how a minister friend and I went to California, and my friend wanted to visit a historic Pentecostal church. The church had been home to great revivals in the past. We got to the building and went inside. As soon as we got in, he said, "It's a dinosaur. Let's go."

I was like, "Is that it? You came in for that?"

"That's it. It's a dinosaur. Let's go."

It's terrible to call a church a dinosaur. The church had a revival years ago, but now there was no glory, no presence, no weight, no springs, no water, and no Spirit. Water represents the Holy Ghost. At this church there was no flow of the Spirit, no fountain of the Holy Ghost, no new songs flowing, no prophetic utterances, and no revelation. There was nothing fresh happening there that would lead you to think about a spring.

A spring always gives fresh water. It is not stale. If there's no fountain, no spring, the water becomes stagnant, and when it becomes stagnant, it becomes stale. It becomes a swamp. Zion, don't end up in a swamp church. Most of all don't end up with a swamp heart.

In a swamp nothing flows. Everything sits still. There are alli-gators, crocodiles, swamp monsters, and creatures from the Black Lagoon—you name it.

There was a program on television called *Swamp People*. My wife used to watch it. It is part of a trend of reality shows that have become so popular. On the show the people go and kill crocodiles and alligators. Yes, they catch them, and that's how they make money.

I don't do swamps, so this is not my calling. I have the blood of Jesus. I am not a swamp man. Some people love swamps. They have their boat on the swamp. Not me. Swamps symbolize water both in condition and direction that is opposite the river of God. It is stagnant. There is no flow, no movement, no fountain, and no spring. It is a swamp.

But thank God for Zion, where there is a river whose streams make glad the city of our God. Zion has a spring, a fountain of life always flowing with something fresh, something new, and something that brings life.

God wants a fountain to flow in your life. You should never be dry, dead, barren, parched, and thirsty. Out of your belly shall flow rivers of living water. The prophetic—being able to speak and hear the word of the Lord—should always be bubbling up and flowing. There should always a freshness flowing free in Zion—new songs, new words, new visions, and new dreams.

Chapter 5

ZION HEART

And I have put my words in thy mouth, and I have covered thee in the shadow of mine hand, that I may plant the heavens, and lay the foundations of the earth, and say unto Zion, Thou art my people.
—ISAIAH 51:16

ZION HEART IS a term I first heard while listening to a message on Zion by Kevin Leal at one of our Asaph Worship Gatherings. I love to hear prophets preach and teach the Word because there's an anointing on prophets to look at Scriptures from an uncommon perspective. When I preach on Zion, I preach it from an apostolic perspective. Hearing his prophetic approach to the topic was very unusual and refreshing. I told him I felt like the Joker in *Batman* when he said, "Where does he get all those wonderful toys?" Prophets receive unusual and amazing insights from God when they study the Scriptures.

As Kevin and I discussed this topic further, we spoke about how the church is limited in its understanding of Zion when it sees it as only a physical place. Zion is in fact a people and then not just a people—Zion is also a heart attitude. Zion is not limited to the types and shadows of the old covenant. The reality of Zion has been made full in Christ. Zion, which is the kingdom, which is the church, is in our hearts. God once dwelled in a physical temple; now we are the temple of God (1 Cor. 3:16). "The Most High does not dwell in temples made with hands" (Acts 7:48, NKJV).

It's very seldom that any preacher preaches on Zion because to most Christians Zion is a future reality, not something we can experience in the present. When you have a revelation of this subject, it gives you insight on who you are as a son or daughter of God. Zion is not a physical location, Zion is a people, and Zion was, of course, the place of worship.

Two thousand years ago Jesus said, "The hour cometh, and now is" (John 4:23). He said this to the Samaritan woman He met one day at a well. He was letting her know that a time was coming when people would no longer worship at the temple in Jerusalem but would worship in spirit and in truth. Jesus was taking the focus off the physical location, saying that act of worship was temporary. As a matter of fact He was letting her know the temple would be destroyed, but God seeks, looks for, and searches for people who will worship Him in spirit and in truth.

God is always looking and searching for worshippers who worship Him in spirit by the Holy Ghost. This is why I emphasize prophetic worship so much. People may wonder why I have such a passion for this. It's because the Spirit-filled worship is not depending on the songs you know. It does not depend on what someone else sings, what's popular, or who has the greatest song out. Spirit-filled worship depends on the Spirit of God.

Unfortunately not many people want to do what it takes to draw from the Holy Ghost. So many of us are lazy. We don't want to use our faith. We don't want to move in the Spirit. We'd rather do it the easy way. We'd rather do the big things everyone else is doing—the sound, the song. There may be a lot of great sounds and great songs. I'm not against great anointed songs, but nothing takes the place of the Holy Ghost. Nothing. You get breakthroughs and miracles when you move in the Spirit that you do not get by copying someone else. And a lot of people don't want it. They go after what's popular—lights, camera, action, smoke…Looks good, sounds good, but it will never replace the power and grace that comes through the Holy Ghost.

When you learn how to live in and move in the Spirit, get ready for some blessings that normal people don't get. Unusual things happen. Special breakthroughs happen in your life. It's a different lifestyle. It's the lifestyle of one whose heart is toward Zion—one who loves the unadulterated presence of God, one whose heart is for God and His heart is for them. And once you get used to this level of worship and relationship, you can't go back.

GOD'S HEART FOR ZION

Psalm 87:2 says, "The LORD loveth the gates of Zion more than all the dwellings of Jacob." God has a special love for Zion; He loves it more than any other place. If you want to know what God loves, what pleases Him, and what excites Him—it's Zion. He loves the gates of Zion more than every other place in the land and every other city, whether it's Bethlehem or Nazareth. His love for no other place can compare to the love God has for Zion. There is something special about Zion that God chooses, loves, favors, and takes pleasure in. So if I am a Zion-hearted believer who knows God loves Zion, I need to make sure I am in the place God loves. I need to make sure I am among the people whom God loves. Because when it says God loves Zion, it means He favors Zion.

If you want the favor of God on your life, realize God looks at Zion, and says, "Now, that's what I like. That's what I choose. That's what I love and favor. That's what I bless. Those are the people who are special to me: Zion people, worshippers, prophetic people, glory people, dancers, people who love my presence."

Not tradition, not a religion, and not a denomination—God doesn't choose those things. He doesn't choose what man chooses. People like all kinds of stuff, but I want to like what God likes. God loves the beauty of Zion, so if God loves Zion, there should be something in me that also loves Zion and its ways. If the Spirit of God is in you and God loves Zion, then you should also love Zion. You should love praise and worship. You should love the presence of God and His glory. You should love the song of the Lord and new songs. You should love the prophetic. You should love dancing, celebrating, and enjoying His glory. You should love Zion as He loves Zion.

To love Zion, you have to be born in Zion. Like the man written of in Psalm 87:4–5, Zion is your city. When you get born again, you are born in a heavenly city. We discussed this in chapter 3. You may be physically born in Chicago, but there's a birth that supersedes your birth in Chicago—it's your birth into Zion. When you are birthed in Zion, Zion is birthed in you. Once you get birthed in Zion and born of it, Zion becomes your city, and you won't be satisfied to live anywhere else.

In the natural you never forget the place you were born, no matter where else you may live. You never forget how you came into the earth—what city, what country, or what town you were born in. It's your native land. You may load up the truck and move to Beverly Hills, but you are still a hillbilly at heart.

A People Called Zion

The people of Zion have a heart for Zion. Zion has been birthed in their hearts, and they love it more than any other place, just as God does. To get a picture of what a Zion heart looks like, let's look at a few characteristics of what it is from Scripture.

David embodies the Zion heart. He is the first one who always comes to my mind as he is the one God anointed to set a pattern for worship that still leads the body of Christ today. He had a heart after God and a heart for Zion. We know more about David's heart than that of any other person in Scripture. David reveals his heart through the many psalms he wrote and sang. Zion is called the city of David. David is the only person in Scripture called a man after God's heart (1 Sam. 13:14).

God loved David's heart. God also loves Zion. Just as we should pay attention to what God loves, we should also learn and model the characteristics of the people God loves.

> And when he had removed him, he raised up unto them David to be their king; to whom also he gave their testimony, and said, I have found David the son of Jesse, a man after mine own heart, which shall fulfil all my will.
>
> —Acts 13:22

The following verse gives us a clue about the focus of David's heart. David was concerned about fulfilling the will of God.

> I delight to do thy will, O my God: yea, thy law is within my heart.
>
> —Psalm 40:8

Zion is a part of the will of God. It was always the will of God for Zion to be in the earth.

Those who have a Zion heart love Zion. They are born in and dwell in Zion, and Zion dwells in them. They are a part of Zion, and they fellowship with others who love Zion.

Jesus is the chief cornerstone of Zion. Jesus, the rejected stone, became the head of the corner. The Zion heart trusts in Jesus, the chief cornerstone. The cornerstone is the foundation stone. The Zion heart has its foundation in Christ. Zion believers build their life on this foundation.

> Wherefore also it is contained in the scripture, Behold, I lay in Sion a chief corner stone, elect, precious: and he that believeth on him shall not be confounded.
>
> —1 Peter 2:6

> The stone which the builders refused is become the head stone of the corner.
>
> —Psalm 118:22

Zion is special to God. Therefore you have a special place in God's heart because you are Zion.

But as we saw in an earlier chapter, you cannot be a citizen of Zion without being born of Zion. The psalmist emphasizes this birth in Psalm 87:5:

> And of Zion it shall be said, This man and that man was born in her: and the highest himself shall establish her.

Then God will prefer you as He prefers Zion. As He has chosen Zion for His habitation, He chooses you.

> For the LORD hath chosen Zion; he hath desired it for his habitation.
>
> —PSALM 132:13

Paul expands the definition of Zion (heavenly) as the church.

> But you have come to Mount Zion and to the city of the living God, the heavenly Jerusalem, to an innumerable company of angels, to the general assembly and church of the firstborn who are registered in heaven, to God the Judge of all, to the spirits of just men made perfect.
>
> —HEBREWS 12:22–23, NKJV

This is not a natural birth but a spiritual birth. This connects Zion to the kingdom. Jesus spoke about being born from above to see the kingdom. This is not a fleshly birth, as I said, but a spiritual birth.

> Jesus answered and said unto him, Verily, verily, I say unto thee, Except a man be born again, he cannot see the kingdom of God.
>
> —JOHN 3:3

Zion has nothing to do with the flesh or natural birth. It has everything to do with the heart because Zion is not earthly. Zion is heavenly and spiritual. Zion is, therefore, the new creation. The new creation was always the goal of the ages. The arrival of the kingdom and heavenly Zion was God's plan from the beginning.

A Zion heart loves to rejoice.

Zion is a place of rejoicing. Those with Zion hearts love to rejoice.

> That I may shew forth all thy praise in the gates of the daughter of Zion: I will rejoice in thy salvation.
>
> —Psalm 9:14

Gladness and joy are in Zion. The daughters also are free in Zion to rejoice. Zion believers understand the judgments of God.

> Let mount Zion rejoice, let the daughters of Judah be glad, because of thy judgments.
>
> —Psalm 48:11

> Zion heard, and was glad; and the daughters of Judah rejoiced because of thy judgments, O Lord.
>
> —Psalm 97:8

A Zion heart is submitted to the King.

Zion is the place of God's rule and reign. A Zion heart is a heart submitted to the King. Rebellion and disobedience do not operate in the Zion heart.

> The Lord shall reign for ever, even thy God, O Zion, unto all generations. Praise ye the Lord.
>
> —Psalm 146:10

A Zion heart loves the next generation.

Zion is multigenerational. Zion is unto all generations. Young and old dwell in Zion. Those with Zion hearts love the next generation. Zion is never obsolete or outmoded. Zion is always current and on the cutting edge.

I have seen many churches and movements lose the Zion heart. These groups become like the old wineskins Christ spoke about in Mark 2:22. These movements become bound by religion and tradition. They become irrelevant to the current generation because they do not continue to renew and revive.

The Zion heart loves renewal. The Zion heart loves the new wine.

> Yet have I set my king upon my holy hill of Zion.
>
> —Psalm 2:6

A Zion heart worships and honors the King.

Zion is the place of the King and His kingdom. Zion is a place where the King is recognized and celebrated. Those with Zion hearts worship and honor the King.

> The Lord shall send the rod of thy strength out of Zion: rule thou in the midst of thine enemies.
>
> —Psalm 110:2

A Zion heart challenges the powers of darkness.

Zion is the place of the King's rule. Zion churches believe in and exercise dominion. The Zion heart is not a defeated heart. Jesus rules in the midst of Zion. Those with Zion hearts challenge the powers of darkness. They rebuke and cast out demons.

> So shall the king greatly desire thy beauty: for he is thy Lord; and worship thou him.
>
> —Psalm 45:11

A Zion heart is the resting place for the presence of God.

Zion is the place of the ark, God's presence. David brought the ark to Zion.

> Then Solomon assembled the elders of Israel, and all the heads of the tribes, the chief of the fathers of the children of Israel, unto Jerusalem, to bring up the ark of the covenant of the Lord out of the city of David, which is Zion.
>
> —2 Chronicles 5:2

The Zion heart loves the ark of God. The ark is the place of glory. The glory of God was spent between the cherubim above the mercy seat.

God shines in Zion. Shining is a picture of glory, splendor, light, and brilliance.[1]

> Give ear, O Shepherd of Israel, thou that leadest Joseph like a flock; thou that dwellest between the cherubims, shine forth.
>
> —Psalm 80:1

David desired a place for God to rest, and he brought the ark to Zion, which is God's resting place forever. The presence of God rests forever in the hearts of Zion believers. The ark would no longer be carried from place to place as during the days of the tabernacle of Moses. The ark found a resting place in Zion.

> This is my rest for ever: here will I dwell; for I have desired it.
>
> —Psalm 132:14

> Arise, O Lord, into thy rest; thou, and the ark of thy strength.
>
> —Psalm 132:8

The word of the Lord is in the tongue of the one with a Zion heart.

David had the Spirit of God upon him, and the word of the Lord was in his tongue. The families of Asaph, Heman, and Jeduthun were prophetic families who played instruments and sang prophetically.

> The Spirit of the Lord spake by me, and his word was in my tongue.
>
> —2 Samuel 23:2

The Zion heart overflows with the word of the Lord. It overflows with new songs. It overflows with prophetic utterances.

> My heart is inditing a good matter: I speak of the things which I have made touching the king: my tongue is the pen of a ready writer.
>
> —Psalm 45:1

> My heart overflows with a goodly theme; I address my psalm to a King. My tongue is like the pen of a ready writer.
>
> —Psalm 45:1, ampc

The heavens drop at the presence of God. Zion is the place of God's presence. Prophetic words and songs drop from heaven when we are in His presence (glory).

The earth shook, the heavens also dropped at the presence of
God: even Sinai itself was moved at the presence of God, the
God of Israel.

—Psalm 68:8

Dropped is the Hebrew word *nataph*, meaning "to drop, drip,
distill, prophesy, preach, discourse," "to drop (prophecy)," "to ooze,"
"distill gradually."[2] The Lord drops His prophetic word from
heaven as a result of His presence. This happens during worship.
God inhabits the praises of His people (Ps. 22:3). The presence of
the Lord will manifest as a result of praise. The presence of God
causes us to worship. Worship is our response to His presence.

God drops the prophetic song. The singers can sing prophetically as a result of nataph. These are songs dropped from heaven.
These songs can drop on anyone in the congregation.

> Another Hebrew word translated "prophet" shows that
> prophets speak what they hear from God (or today from
> the Lord Jesus), and they do not speak on their own. The
> Hebrew word *nataph*, sometimes translated "prophet,"
> means "to drop, drip, or distill." Its uses include rain distilling and dripping from the sky, words that "drop" out of
> someone's mouth, and wine dripping from the mountains in
> Paradise. Although prophets are called upon to "drop" words
> where and when God demands, the more obvious thing we
> learn from *nataph* is that God drops His words upon the
> prophet. It means, as *Strong's Concordance* says, "to speak by
> inspiration." This means that the message the prophet brings
> is not his own message, but the Lord's words, and furthermore it implies that many times the prophet may not know
> much of the message when he starts prophesying, but that
> the words "drop" upon him, i.e., he speaks them as he gets
> them from God.[3]

This dropping also causes us to sing inspired songs. Songs of
inspiration are prophetic songs. The singer is inspired by God to

sing a new song. Churches must allow God to drop these songs during worship. We should not quench the manifestation of the Spirit (1 Thess. 5:19).

This form of singing develops gradually as we ascend in worship, which reflects the meaning of *nataph* I pointed out above—"to distill gradually."

> This form of prophecy distills gradually in your spirit. The Hebrew word *nataph* means a forming, developing word, like ruminating on food. This form of prophetic utterance is slow to develop and comes like the dawn. It is possible to write such inspiration down and deliver it. An example of this is found in Job, "After I had spoken, they spoke no more; my utterance fell gently on their ears" (Job 29:22). As he spoke, they had unfolding revelation or understanding of God's word to them.[4]

Distill means "to appear slowly or in small quantities at a time."[5] This cannot be rushed. It will take some time for these songs to be released. It will take some quality time in worship.

> The prophet's words often revealed the gentle heart of God, their words "distilled and dropped like dew and gentle rain;" "nataph;" 5179. Strong says "nataph," means; "to ooze, i.e., distil gradually; by implication, to fall in drops; and figuratively, to speak by inspiration: drop, prophesy." This word not only shows the gentle side and nature of prophecy; it also reveals that prophecy can come slowly, bit by bit, with pauses, short or long, between the parts of each complete revelation.[6]

The word of the Lord drops in Zion, and Zion believers hear God's Word, speak it, sing it, and obey it.

Zion-hearted believers are diverse.

Zion believers are worldwide. Those with Zion hearts are from every nation and cultural group. Although they come from different backgrounds, they have similar hearts.

All nations whom thou hast made shall come and worship
before thee, O Lord; and shall glorify thy name.

—Psalm 86:9

Zion-hearted believers trust in the Lord.

Remember Zion was a fortress, a stronghold, a castle. Zion was
a mountain fortress that the Jebusites had held up to the time of
David. Zion is the stronghold of God.

And the inhabitants of Jebus said to David, Thou shalt not
come hither. Nevertheless David took the castle of Zion,
which is the city of David.

—1 Chronicles 11:5

Heavenly Zion is impenetrable. Zion is a place of safety and
protection. Those with Zion hearts put their trust in the God
of Zion. The Zion heart is the trusting heart. It is the heart that
depends upon and trusts in the Lord.

They that trust in the Lord shall be as mount Zion, which
cannot be removed, but abideth for ever.

—Psalm 125:1

The psalmist had a Zion heart. David had a Zion heart. The
psalms are filled with references to trusting the Lord. I believe
trusting in the Lord is one major characteristic of the Zion heart.

But let all those that put their trust in thee rejoice: let them
ever shout for joy, because thou defendest them: let them
also that love thy name be joyful in thee.

—Psalm 5:11

In other words, the Lord is my rock and fortress (Zion). The
Zion heart does not trust in the flesh. The Zion heart puts its trust
in God, not in man.

The Lord is my rock, and my fortress, and my deliverer; my
God, my strength, in whom I will trust; my buckler, and the
horn of my salvation, and my high tower.

—Psalm 18:2

O taste and see that the Lord is good: blessed is the man that trusteth in him.

—Psalm 34:8

The Zion heart commits its way unto the Lord and trusts in Him. This means to submit your plans to Him.

Commit thy way unto the Lord; trust also in him; and he shall bring it to pass.

—Psalm 37:5

The Zion heart hates pride. The Zion heart does not respect the proud and arrogant. God hates pride. Pride is an abomination to him.

Blessed is that man that maketh the Lord his trust, and respecteth not the proud, nor such as turn aside to lies.

—Psalm 40:4

The Zion heart trusts in God's mercy.

But I am like a green olive tree in the house of God: I trust in the mercy of God for ever and ever.

—Psalm 52:8

Zion-hearted believers are fearless.

The Zion heart is not afraid of what flesh can do. This is another major characteristic of the Zion heart. David was a man with a Zion heart. He consistently spoke about not fearing man.

In God I will praise his word, in God I have put my trust; I will not fear what flesh can do unto me.

—Psalm 56:4

The Lord is on my side; I will not fear: what can man do unto me.

—Psalm 118:6

Zion believers are not afraid of war. Those with Zion hearts do not fear the enemy. There is no fear of man. The fear of man brings a snare (Prov. 29:25).

Though an host should encamp against me, my heart shall not fear: though war should rise against me, in this will I be confident.

—Psalm 27:3

The Zion heart has God's strength. Zion is a place of strength and might. Fearlessness is a sign of a Zion heart.

The Lord is my light and my salvation; whom shall I fear? the Lord is the strength of my life; of whom shall I be afraid?

—Psalm 27:1

Zion-hearted believers are unshakable.

The Zion heart is established, steadfast, and unshakable.

His heart is established, he shall not be afraid, until he see his desire upon his enemies.

—Psalm 112:8

Surely he shall not be moved for ever: the righteous shall be in everlasting remembrance.

—Psalm 112:6

Zion is an unmovable place. Zion is a mountain and cannot be shaken. Those with Zion hearts are not shaken. God is in the midst of Zion, and Zion cannot be moved.

God is in the midst of her; she shall not be moved: God shall help her, and that right early.

—Psalm 46:5

Those with Zion hearts set the Lord before them always. The Zion heart cannot be moved.

I have set the Lord always before me: because he is at my right hand, I shall not be moved.

—Psalm 16:8

Those with Zion hearts believe in the Lord's protection. The Lord is their defense. The Zion heart is not moved with fear of calamity.

He only is my rock and my salvation: he is my defence; I shall not be moved.

—Psalm 62:6

Zion-hearted believers are pure-hearted.

The Zion heart is a pure heart. It is a heart with no guile.

Blessed is the man unto whom the Lord imputeth not iniquity, and in whose spirit there is no guile.

—Psalm 32:2

Guile is cunningness, slyness, deceit, or craftiness.[7] True worshippers have no guile. Jesus identified Nathaniel as an Israelite indeed, a man with no guile. Jesus had no guile.

Jesus saw Nathanael coming to him, and saith of him, Behold an Israelite indeed, in whom is no guile.

—John 1:47

Psalm 24 describes the person who can ascend the hill of the Lord. It is the person with clean hands and a pure heart. Zion is the hill of God.

Who shall ascend into the hill of the Lord? or who shall stand in his holy place? He that hath clean hands, and a pure heart; who hath not lifted up his soul unto vanity, nor sworn deceitfully. He shall receive the blessing from the Lord, and righteousness from the God of his salvation.

—Psalm 24:3–5

Israel would go up to Zion. They would ascend on their journey. This is because Zion was located in a high place.

Zion-hearted believers walk in truth.

The Zion heart is a truthful heart. Zion believers hate lies.

Lord, who shall abide in thy tabernacle? who shall dwell in thy holy hill? He that walketh uprightly, and worketh righteousness, and speaketh the truth in his heart. He that

backbiteth not with his tongue, nor doeth evil to his neighbour, nor taketh up a reproach against his neighbour.

—Psalm 15:1–3

Zion believers walk in truth. They love the truth of the Word.
They do not compromise when they know truth.

Teach me thy way, O Lord; I will walk in thy truth: unite
my heart to fear thy name.

—Psalm 86:11

For thy lovingkindness is before mine eyes: and I have walked
in thy truth.

—Psalm 26:3

Light and truth is what brings us to Zion.

O send out thy light and thy truth: let them lead me; let
them bring me unto thy holy hill, and to thy tabernacles.

—Psalm 43:3

God desires truth in the inward parts. Truth is not just in the
mouth but in the heart.

Behold, thou desirest truth in the inward parts: and in the
hidden part thou shalt make me to know wisdom.

—Psalm 51:6

There is a banner of truth. Truth must be lifted high.

Thou hast given a banner to them that fear thee, that it may
be displayed because of the truth. Selah.

—Psalm 60:4

God's truth is to be praised.

For his merciful kindness is great toward us: and the truth of
the Lord endureth for ever. Praise ye the Lord.

—Psalm 117:2

Truth is one thing that motivates the Zion believers to praise
and worship.

I will worship toward thy holy temple, and praise thy name
for thy lovingkindness and for thy truth: for thou hast mag-
nified thy word above all thy name.

—PSALM 138:2

Zion is called the city of truth. You cannot be a part of Zion
and not love truth.

Thus saith the LORD; I am returned unto Zion, and will
dwell in the midst of Jerusalem: and Jerusalem shall be
called a city of truth; and the mountain of the LORD of hosts
the holy mountain.

—ZECHARIAH 8:3

Zion-hearted believers have a heart for salvation and deliverance.

Zion is a place of salvation and deliverance.

Behold, the LORD hath proclaimed unto the end of the world,
Say ye to the daughter of Zion, Behold, thy salvation cometh;
behold, his reward is with him, and his work before him.

—ISAIAH 62:11

Salvation is in Zion. Zion churches preach salvation. Zion
believers emphasize salvation. The Zion heart is a heart of salvation.

But upon mount Zion shall be deliverance, and there shall
be holiness; and the house of Jacob shall possess their
possessions.

—OBADIAH 17

One of the first messages I ever preached about deliverance was
from this verse in Obadiah. Notice the progression. After deliverance comes holiness and then the ability to possess our possessions.

Salvation is deliverance. Deliverance was an important part of
the ministry of Christ. Jesus cast out devils with the finger of God
(Luke 11:20). The casting out of devils was a sign of the arrival
of the kingdom. Jesus cast out spirits with His word (Matt. 8:16).
Jesus cast out many devils (Mark 1:34). The disciples cast out many

devils (Mark 6:13). Jesus cast seven devils out of Mary Magdalene (Mark 16:9).

The deliverance ministry of Christ was a notable part of His ministry. It was something so new (Mark 1:27) that when He began to do it, the religious leaders accused Him of casting out devils by Beelzebub (Matt. 12:24). Jesus preached and cast out devils wherever He went (Mark 1:39).

Multitudes came to Jesus for deliverance. Devils came out of many (Luke 4:41). Deliverance is the children's bread (Matt. 15:26). Every believer has a right to deliverance, and Zion is the place of deliverance.

Many spirits in people need to be challenged and cast out. The most common demons are rejection, rebellion, bitterness, pride, lust, fear, hurt, anger, confusion, infirmity, witchcraft, and hatred. Jesus gives us power and authority to heal the sick and cast out devils (Luke 9:1).

The healing and deliverance ministries are often connected. Many sicknesses have demonic roots. People brought the sick and demonized to Jesus for healing (Mark 1:32). The deliverance ministry is a miracle ministry (Mark 9:38–40).

Jesus, the Deliverer, comes out of Zion. He brings salvation. He turned ungodliness from Jacob. Jesus, the Deliverer, is connected to Zion.

> And so all Israel shall be saved: as it is written, There shall come out of Sion the Deliverer, and shall turn away ungodliness from Jacob.
> —ROMANS 11:26

Saviors (deliverers) are raised up in Zion. Zion churches are churches of deliverance. We are seeing many deliverance workers and teams being raised in many churches. Zion judges Esau. Esau is a picture of the flesh and the demonic.

And saviours shall come up on mount Zion to judge the mount of Esau; and the kingdom shall be the LORD's.

—OBADIAH 21

The Zion heart is a heart that loves freedom and liberty. The Zion heart hates bondage. You are Zion. You cast out devils. You walk in freedom and liberty. You are delivered, and you are a deliverer. You have been set free, and you set those free who are in bondage.

Zion-hearted believers preach the good news.

Zion churches love the good news. Zion believers publish peace. The Zion heart is a heart with glad tidings. Zion believers declare God reigns.

How beautiful upon the mountains are the feet of him that bringeth good tidings, that publisheth peace; that bringeth good tidings of good, that publisheth salvation; that saith unto Zion, Thy God reigneth.

—ISAIAH 52:7

You are Zion. You preach the good news. You declare the rule and reign of Christ. Zion proclaims the good news of the kingdom.

Zion-hearted believers have a heart for restoration.

Health, healing, and restoration are in Zion. The Zion heart is a heart of restoration. Zion churches and believers believe in restoration.

For I will restore health unto thee, and I will heal thee of thy wounds, saith the LORD; because they called thee an Outcast, saying, This is Zion, whom no man seeketh after.

—JEREMIAH 30:17

Earthly Zion was rejected because of its disobedience and rebellion. Zion went into captivity because of covenant disobedience. God restores Zion through Messiah. Salvation, healing, and deliverance came to Zion.

The Zion heart loves the rejected and the outcast. Zion churches bring deliverance and healing to the rejected.

Zion-hearted believers love to meet with God.

Zion believers love to appear before God. The Zion heart loves to meet God and see His face.

> They go from strength to strength, every one of them in Zion appeareth before God.
> —Psalm 84:7

> My soul thirsteth for God, for the living God: when shall I come and appear before God?
> —Psalm 42:2

The Zion heart welcomes examination. Zion believers are open and honest before the Lord. Zion believers are transparent. The Zion heart is a transparent heart.

> Examine me, O Lord, and prove me; try my reins and my heart.
> —Psalm 26:2

Zion-hearted believers have the favor of God.

Zion enjoys God's favor. Zion believers walk in divine favor. A revelation of favor will change your life.

> Thou shalt arise, and have mercy upon Zion: for the time to favour her, yea, the set time, is come.
> —Psalm 102:13

God favored Zion over every city. God chose Zion. God redeemed and restored Zion because of favor. Favor is grace. You are Zion. Grace is multiplied in your life.

You are favored by God. I call this the force of favor. Favor will dramatically change your life and cause great breakthroughs. Favor releases mercy. Mercy is God's lovingkindness.

Favor is one of my favorite subjects in Scripture. Many things attract the favor of God. Humility, wisdom, righteousness, prayer, worship, faith, and giving can all attract favor to you like a magnet.

Glory is also a favor magnet. Zion is a place of favor. I define *favor* as God's willingness to use His power and ability on your behalf.

David received favor. Favor gave him victory (Ps. 41:11). Favor can surround you like a shield (Ps. 5:12). Favor can last a lifetime (Ps. 30:5). Favor caused his mountain to stand strong (Ps. 30:7). Favor causes promotion (Ps. 89:17). You need to confess favor. Some favor confessions are at the end of this chapter, which you can use daily to increase the favor of God in your life.

Zion-hearted believers are glory carriers.

The Lord builds up Zion. The Lord appears in his glory in Zion. Zion churches are filled with glory.

> When the Lord shall build up Zion, he shall appear in his glory.
>
> —Psalm 102:16

Isaiah chapter 60 describes the glory of Zion. This chapter is filled with amazing truths concerning Zion. The characteristics of Zion include shining, elevation, wealth, attraction, beauty, sons and daughters (posterity), excellence, upgrade, restoration, increase, abundance, multiplication, strength, peace (shalom), light, revelation, honor, favor, and blessing.

Zion believers are glory carriers. The Zion heart is committed to God's glory. The Zion heart gives God glory.

> Give unto the Lord, ye kindreds of the people, give unto the Lord glory and strength.
>
> —Psalm 96:7

Zion-hearted believers are givers.

> Give unto the Lord the glory due unto his name: bring an offering, and come into his courts.
>
> —Psalm 96:8

Zion believers are givers. They bring offerings and honor the Lord. The come into his courts with sacrifice. The Zion heart is a sacrificial heart.

Zion-hearted believers have a heart for joyful prayer.

> Even them will I bring to my holy mountain, and make them joyful in my house of prayer: their burnt offerings and their sacrifices shall be accepted upon mine altar; for mine house shall be called an house of prayer for all people.
>
> —Isaiah 56:7

Zion is the place for joyful, strong prayer. Zion churches are praying churches. Isaiah 56 is a word that encourages strangers and eunuchs to come to Zion. They would have a place in God's house. They could come with prayer and sacrifice to the holy mountain.

Prayer is joyful in Zion. Prayer is not a struggle. Prayer is not something we do because of religion. Prayer is enjoyed in Zion. Zion is the place for intercessors and praying prophets. You are Zion. You are joyful in prayer.

The house of prayer would be for all nations. Jesus spoke this verse when He drove the moneychangers out of the temple (Matt. 21:12). People were not attracted to the temple because of what was taking place there. The blind and lame came to the temple, and He healed them.

This is a word to the outcast. God accepts them and gives them a name in Zion. Zion is a place for the rejected and outcast. This is what I love about Zion. Zion opens its gates to people that other cities would reject.

Then they not only come to Zion, but they also are joyful in prayer. Their sacrifices are accepted. Prayer is a privilege and honor for all who come to Zion. God not only welcomed the Jews, but also He welcomed the foreigners and the eunuchs.

> Neither let the son of the stranger, that hath joined himself to the Lord, speak, saying, The Lord hath utterly separated me from his people: neither let the eunuch say, Behold, I am a dry tree.
>
> —Isaiah 56:3

A dry tree is an emblem of that which is barren, useless, unfruitful. By the Law of Moses such persons could not be enrolled or numbered in the congregation of the Lord (Deut. 23:2). The sense here is that they should not hereafter be subjected to religious and civil disabilities. These external barriers to the full privileges among the people of God would be removed. All classes and ranks would be admitted to the same privileges; all would be on the same level.[8]

Zion-hearted believers love the ways of God.

Zion is the mountain of God. Zion is the place where we learn the ways of God and how to walk in His paths. The Zion heart loves the ways of God and the paths of God.

> And it shall come to pass in the last days, that the mountain of the LORD's house shall be established in the top of the mountains, and shall be exalted above the hills; and all nations shall flow unto it. And many people shall go and say, Come ye, and let us go up to the mountain of the LORD, to the house of the God of Jacob; and he will teach us of his ways, and we will walk in his paths: for out of Zion shall go forth the law, and the word of the LORD from Jerusalem.
>
> —ISAIAH 2:2–3

This is the cry of the Zion heart: to know and walk in God's paths. The Scriptures have much to say about the path you take in life. Your paths determine your destination and your walk.

You are Zion. God will teach you His paths.

> Shew me thy ways, O LORD; teach me thy paths.
>
> —PSALM 25:4

You are Zion. You walk in His ways, and you are blessed.

> Blessed is every one that feareth the LORD; that walketh in his ways.
>
> —PSALM 128:1

You are Zion. God will keep you from slipping.

Hold up my goings in thy paths, that my footsteps slip not.

—Psalm 17:5

You are Zion. God leads you into the right paths.

He restoreth my soul: he leadeth me in the paths of righteousness for his name's sake.

—Psalm 23:3

You are Zion. God will show you the path of life.

Thou wilt shew me the path of life: in thy presence is fulness of joy; at thy right hand there are pleasures for evermore.

—Psalm 16:11

Zion believers are restorers of paths to dwell in. Abandoned paths are opened again through Zion believers. We rebuild the old waste. We raise up the foundations of many generations. We repair the breach. This is another picture of rebuilding and restoration. You are Zion. You have been restored. Your breaches have been repaired.

And they that shall be of thee shall build the old waste places: thou shalt raise up the foundations of many generations; and thou shalt be called, The repairer of the breach, The restorer of paths to dwell in.

—Isaiah 58:12

The Zion heart loves the straight paths. The Zion heart hates crooked paths. The Zion heart loves the paths of mercy, righteousness, and truth.

And make straight paths for your feet, lest that which is lame be turned out of the way; but let it rather be healed.

—Hebrews 12:13

The Zion heart is a perfect heart. The word *perfect* in the verse below means "complete" and "whole."[9]

God searches the earth for the Zion heart.

> For the eyes of the LORD run to and fro throughout the
> whole earth, to shew himself strong in the behalf of them
> whose heart is perfect toward him.
>
> —2 CHRONICLES 16:9

God shows Himself strong on the behalf of those with Zion hearts.

> I will behave myself wisely in a perfect way. O when wilt
> thou come unto me? I will walk within my house with a per-
> fect heart.
>
> —PSALM 101:2

ZION BELIEVERS ARE GOD'S FAVORITES

God loves the gates of Zion, which means when you're in Zion, God looks at you differently. There's a special love He has for you. I know we've been taught God loves everybody the same, but the Bible said, "Jacob have I loved, but Esau have I hated" (Rom. 9:13).

I know we want to believe God loves everybody the same, but He doesn't. God loved David. He rejected Saul. I know God is love. I understand that, but God has favorites. Not to say God is a respecter of persons, but God doesn't respect you based on who you are. You don't impress God. But God does have favorites, and God chooses.

It's the same with how you have favorite foods. When you prepare to order a meal, you don't look at the menu and just say, "Bring me anything." You choose what you like. You love certain foods, and you choose those.

God chooses and favors Zion. When you get in Zion, there's a special love you get to experience all your life. God will move for you, fight for you, and bless you. God will promote you. God will pass over others to get to you because He sees Zion. That's what I'm looking for.

If you want those special, unusual blessings, if you want to get whatever is not common, and if you want to receive more than common blessings, then you must be born of Zion. God blesses a lot of people. He reigns on the just and unjust. But, again, if you want those uncommon blessings, those choice blessings, and if you want the finest of the wheat, you can't be like everybody else. You can't sing like everybody else. You can't talk like everybody else. You can't worship like everybody else. You have to get in Zion.

If you want to go to that next level, where God favors, chooses, promotes, and blesses you—the place where God multiplies and increases you—then get in Zion. If you want to be where God protects you and looks on you and smiles, then get the heart of Zion. You need to develop a Zion heart if you want to be in a place where God says, "Now that one right there, don't mess with that one. You mess with that one, you'll get in trouble. That's one of my favorites right there. Don't pick a fight with them because I'll fight their battles. Leave that one alone."

The Scripture says God loves the gates of Zion more than all (Ps. 87:2). That means God loves some places more than others, which means He loves the gates of Zion more than all the other dwellings. We may want to think God loves everybody the same, and He loves the wicked just as much as He loves the righteous. I am here to tell you He doesn't. How can that be? You mean to tell me God sees no difference between me and the wicked? Me and the murderer? I'm doing everything to live holy and live clean, and I get the same blessing the murderer gets? No.

The Bible says, "Delight yourself in the LORD; and He will give you the desires of your heart" (Ps. 37:4, NASB), and "No good thing will he withhold from them that walk uprightly" (Ps. 84:11). There is a difference between clean and unclean, holy and unholy, and righteous and unrighteous. There is a difference between one who is a Zion believer and one who is not. Zion heart, I want you to have God's best. I want you to experience special miracles and special breakthroughs. When God sees you, I want His favor and His light to shine on you.

Prayers for a Zion Heart

Lord, give me a Zion heart.

Lord, let Your love be upon my life because I am Zion.

Lord, let me drink from the springs of Zion. Let me be satisfied with the water, the river, and the spirit that flows in Zion.

Lord, I thank You. I have found Zion. I will stay in Zion all the days of my life. I will not leave. It is my resting place.

Lord, let Your blessings come on my life in Zion. Do great things for me, unusual things, and special things because I am Zion. I have a Zion heart.

Lord, give me a revelation of Zion and what it means to be Zion. Let me lead a Zion lifestyle.

Thank You, Lord, for giving me a Zion heart. I believe it today. I confess it today. I receive it today, in Jesus' name.

Confessions for the Favor of Zion

I am Zion.

God favors Zion.

I have favor with God and man.

I have an abundance of favor.

I wear the crown of favor.

I walk in the path of favor.

I wear the coat of favor.

I drink from the fountain of favor.

I harvest from the field of favor.

I live by the river of favor.

I am covered by the flood of favor.

I am overwhelmed by an avalanche of favor.

My cup runs over with favor.

I draw from the well of favor.

I am impacted by the winds of favor.

I am revived by the breath of favor.

I am soaked in the rain of favor.

I live under the cloud of favor.

I am refreshed by the dew of favor.

I am a recipient of the King's favor.

I walk in extraordinary favor.

I live with unusual favor.

I obtain ridiculous favor.

I enjoy extreme favor.

I have a lifetime of favor.

I reap heaps of favor.

I will never lack favor.

I always increase in favor.

I have an anointing for favor.

I have gifts that bring favor.

My relationships are favored.

I am rich with favor.

I have strong faith for favor.

I am surrounded by favor.

Favor locates me.

Favor follows me.

Favor is my portion in life.

I enjoy financial favor.

I have favor in my city.

I have mega favor.

Favor flows out of my life like a river.

I sow favor.

I enjoy new favor.

I receive the Word of favor.

I will sing about favor.

I praise the Lord for favor.

I come to the throne of favor.

I walk in the revelation of favor.

I understand favor.

Wisdom gives me favor.

I associate with those who are favored.

I am highly favored.

Favor is multiplied in my life.

Chapter 6

WORSHIP—THE DOORWAY
TO THE GLORY REALM

*And they brought in the ark of the Lord, and set it in his place,
in the midst of the tabernacle that David had pitched for it: and
David offered burnt offerings and peace offerings before the Lord.*
—2 Samuel 6:17

WORSHIP IS THE doorway to the glory of God, and Zion
believers love the glory. The Zion heart loves true worship.
David had a Zion heart, and David was a worshipper. David established worship in Zion. He set the ark of God under a tent and
appointed the Levitical families of Asaph, Heman, and Jeduthun
to worship with instruments and prophecy (1 Chron. 25). David
established prophetic worship. Israel's worship was established by
David and by the prophets Gad and Nathan (2 Chron. 29:25). The
Zion heart loves the prophetic word and the prophetic song.

After years of ministry and being involved in worship, I have
concluded that musicians and singers should be able to prophesy.
We have separated music from prophecy in many churches, but
they are connected in the Word of God. I have always had a strong
focus on what David established in Zion.

First Chronicles 16:37, 41–42 tells us how David built a prophetic model for praise and worship:

> So he left there before the ark of the covenant of the Lord
> Asaph and his brethren, to minister before the ark continually, as every day's work required....And with them Heman
> and Jeduthun, and the rest that were chosen, who were

expressed by name, to give thanks to the LORD, because his mercy endureth for ever; and with them Heman and Jeduthun with trumpets and cymbals for those that should make a sound, and with musical instruments of God. And the sons of Jeduthun were porters.

In 1 Chronicles 25 David established worship with three prophetic families—the families of Asaph, Heman, and Jeduthun. The fathers of these families were prophets (seers), and their children also prophesied with instruments. David placed Asaph and his brethren before the ark to minister continually. Asaph was a Levitical musician. He and his brethren prophesied with instruments before the ark (1 Chron. 25:1–7).

Many musicians in our churches have never been activated in the prophetic. Many are skillful, but they do not operate in any level of prophecy. This needs to change if we want to see the glory of God in our worship. We need strong musicians able to prophesy. We need singers who can prophesy as well.

David, the worshipper, was also a prophet. God used prophets—David, Gad, and Nathan—to establish Israel's worship.

And he set the Levites in the house of the LORD with cymbals, with psalteries, and with harps, according to the commandment of David, and of Gad the king's seer, and Nathan the prophet: for so was the commandment of the LORD by his prophets.

—2 CHRONICLES 29:25

Musicians and singers, and everyone else, should desire to prophesy (1 Cor. 14:1). It is not enough to just play an instrument or learn and play songs. Musicians and singers need to move by inspiration. A *prophet* is defined simply as an inspired man or woman.[1] To *prophesy* simply means to speak, sing, or play by inspiration.[2]

Unclean musicians have unclean spirits. Spirits, whether clean and uplifting or unclean and demonic, can be transmitted through music as we can see from the example of David playing for Saul.

His music had such a holy influence that it drove out Saul's evil spirits. (See 1 Samuel 16:23.)

Music is a powerful force. Satan targets the musicians. Music affects everyone in the church. Everyone who comes in is exposed to the music. It is wise for intercessors to pray for the music department and even to pray over the musical instruments.

Prophetic musicians understand they are called. This places a greater demand on them to live a lifestyle of holiness. They are not just playing music in a church to receive a salary. It is not just a job for them. It is a divine calling. They need to study the Word, pray, fast, and flow in the spirit like every other believer. It is time to raise the standard. Musicians should play music that the glory of God can indwell.

Prophetic musicians can pull the whole congregation into the prophetic flow. This is what happened in 1 Samuel 10:5–6 when Saul met a company of prophets playing musical instruments and prophesying. Saul, too, began to prophesy in the presence of the Lord among them.

ZION WORSHIP IS GLOBAL

God's desire is for the nations to worship. In other words, worship in Zion would not be limited to a physical place, but it would be worldwide, in every nation, and among all people. The psalmists prophesied the day we are now living in, saying:

> All the ends of the world shall remember and turn unto the LORD: and all the kindreds of the nations shall worship before thee.
>
> —PSALM 22:27

> All the earth shall worship thee, and shall sing unto thee; they shall sing to thy name. Selah.
>
> —PSALM 66:4

> All nations whom thou hast made shall come and worship before thee, O Lord; and shall glorify thy name.
>
> —Psalm 86:9

In other words, Zion would consist of all nations. Worship would be global. There are no geopolitical boundaries to worship. The earth is filled with the knowledge of the glory of the Lord as the waters cover the sea.

BEYOND THE PHYSICAL

Zion was God's choice. God's habitation is no longer a physical place.

> For the Lord hath chosen Zion; he hath desired it for his habitation.
>
> —Psalm 132:13

Zion is God's favored place. David was chosen by God, and so was his city. You are Zion. You are chosen. You are favored. You are the habitation of God through the Spirit. God dwells in us.

Here are some characteristics of what to expect more of as Zion worshippers in the days and years to come.

Zion worshippers have a heart for worship and the prophetic.

> David was dressed in a fine linen robe, as were all the Levites who carried the ark, the Levites who were singers, and Chenaniah, the leader of the musicians' prophetic songs. David also wore a linen ephod.
>
> —1 Chronicles 15:27, gw

David's heart for worship can be seen throughout the psalms. Zion churches are worshipping churches. Zion churches are prophetic churches.

> But as for me, I will come into thy house in the multitude of thy mercy: and in thy fear will I worship toward thy holy temple.
>
> —Psalm 5:7

> Give unto the LORD the glory due unto his name; worship
> the LORD in the beauty of holiness.
>
> —PSALM 29:2

David prophesied this worship would be worldwide with the growth and expansion of the kingdom. I have ministered in over eighty nations, and I have met believers with Zion hearts worldwide.

> All the ends of the world shall remember and turn unto
> the LORD: and all the kindreds of the nations shall worship
> before thee.
>
> —PSALM 22:27

Zion worshippers worship in spirit and in truth.

Although earthly Zion was in Jerusalem, it was never the will of God for it to remain there only. The earthly mountain would be replaced by the spiritual mountain.

> Jesus saith unto her, Woman, believe me, the hour cometh,
> when ye shall neither in this mountain, nor yet at Jerusalem,
> worship the Father....But the hour cometh, and now is,
> when the true worshippers shall worship the Father in spirit
> and in truth: for the Father seeketh such to worship him.
> God is a Spirit: and they that worship him must worship
> him in spirit and in truth.
>
> —JOHN 4:21, 23–24

Earthly Jerusalem would no longer be the place of worship. True worship is in the new Zion. The Zion heart loves worship that is in spirit and truth. Zion is not a place of fleshly worship. Zion is a place of Holy Spirit–led and anointed worship. Zion is the holy hill of God. God seeks worshippers with a Zion heart.

> Exalt the LORD our God, and worship at his holy hill; for the
> LORD our God is holy.
>
> —PSALM 99:9

And it shall be, that whoso will not come up of all the families of the earth unto Jerusalem to worship the King, the LORD of hosts, even upon them shall be no rain.

—ZECHARIAH 14:17

This Jerusalem is the New Jerusalem. Those who do not come to worship receive no rain. The Zion heart believes in the present-day rule and reign of the king. Zion believers believe in the king's majesty, strength, and power. They sing about and declare His majesty and splendor.

The LORD reigneth, he is clothed with majesty; the LORD is clothed with strength, wherewith he hath girded himself: the world also is stablished, that it cannot be moved.

—PSALM 93:1

Zion worshippers love the new song and sound.

Honour and majesty are before him: strength and beauty are in his sanctuary.

—PSALM 96:6

Zion churches and believers sing new songs. The Zion heart loves the new song.

O sing unto the LORD a new song; for he hath done marvellous things: his right hand, and his holy arm, hath gotten him the victory.

—PSALM 98:1

Zion believers not only like new songs, but they like loud sounds as well. Zion is known for its sound. Blessed are the people that know the joyful sound (Ps. 89:15). The glory of God produces a sound.

Sing unto him a new song; play skilfully with a loud noise.

—PSALM 33:3

Zion is a place of instruments. Zion believers like to praise with musical instruments. Zion has singers and instruments. Zion is a source of joy (springs) for Zion believers.

> As well the singers as the players on instruments shall be there: all my springs are in thee.
>
> —Psalm 87:7

> Praise him with the timbrel and dance: praise him with stringed instruments and organs.
>
> —Psalm 150:4

A group of psalms called Psalms of Ascent (Psalms 120–134), were sung by worshippers as they journeyed to Jerusalem for the annual feasts. Israel's natural journey is a picture of our spiritual ascent in worship. Zion churches ascend in worship. The service continues to go higher in degrees as we sing and play instruments. The Zion heart is a pure and ascending heart. Because of their purity of heart, Zion believers ascend in praise. They believe in high praise.

> Let the high praises of God be in their mouth, and a two-edged sword in their hand.
>
> —Psalm 149:6

Zion is also a place of high sound. We praise the Lord in the heights. The Zion heart lives in the heights.

> Praise him upon the loud cymbals: praise him upon the high sounding cymbals.
>
> —Psalm 150:5

> Praise ye the Lord. Praise ye the Lord from the heavens: praise him in the heights.
>
> —Psalm 148:1

Zion is in the heights. We come to the height of Zion.

> Therefore they shall come and sing in the height of Zion, and shall flow together to the goodness of the Lord, for wheat, and for wine, and for oil, and for the young of the flock and

of the herd: and their soul shall be as a watered garden; and
they shall not sorrow any more at all.

—Jeremiah 31:12

Zion worshippers are praisers.

This shall be written for the generation to come: and the
people which shall be created shall praise the Lord.

—Psalm 102:18

There is a people created to praise. The Zion heart is a heart of
praise. This is not surprising considering the earthly Zion is called
the city of David. David was known for his praise. Zion churches are
churches of praise. You do not have a Zion heart if you do not praise.

Sing praises to the Lord, which dwelleth in Zion: declare
among the people his doings.

—Psalm 9:11

Zion believers praise the Lord with their whole hearts.

I will praise thee, O Lord, with my whole heart; I will shew
forth all thy marvellous works.

—Psalm 9:1

Praise is important to Zion. Zion is a place of praise. Zion
believers are praisers. David was a praiser, and he brought praise
to his city. Praise is one major aspect of Zion. There is no Zion
apart from praise.

The word study of *praise* is important to understand the fullness
of this subject. All these aspects of praise are in Zion.

1. *Halal* is a primary Hebrew root word for *praise*. Our
   word *hallelujah* comes from this base word. It means
   "to be clear," "to praise," "to shine," "to boast," "to show,"
   "to celebrate," "to be (clamorously) foolish."[3] Psalm
   113:1: "Praise [halal] ye the Lord, praise [halal] o ye
   servants of the Lord, praise [halal] the name of the
   Lord."

2. *Yadah* is a verb with a root meaning "to revere or worship (with extended hands)."[4] Second Chronicles 20:21: "Give thanks [yadah] to the LORD, for His lovingkindness is everlasting" (NASB).

3. *Towdah* comes from the same principle root word as *yadah* but is used more specifically. *Towdah* means "an extension of the hand, i.e. (by implication) avowal, or (usually) adoration."[5] Psalm 50:14: "Offer unto God praise [towdah] and pay thy vows unto the Most High."

4. *Shabach* means "to laud, praise, commend." This word connotes loud praise. God likes loud praise.[6] Psalm 63:3: "Because thy lovingkindness is better than life, my lips shall praise [shabach] thee."

5. *Barak* means "to kneel; by implication to bless God (as an act of adoration)," "salute."[7] Psalm 95:6: "O come let us worship and bow down; let us kneel [barak] before the LORD our maker."

6. *Zamar* means "to touch the strings or parts of a musical instrument, i.e., play upon it; to make music, accompanied by the voice; hence to celebrate in song and music:—give praise, sing forth praises, psalms."[8] *Zamar* is a Hebrew word that reminds us that God loves instrumental praise. Psalm 21:13: "Be thou exalted, LORD, in thine own strength, so will we sing and praise [zamar] thy power."

7. "*Tehillah* is derived from the word *halal* and means 'the singing of halals, to sing or to laud; perceived to involve music, especially singing; hymns of the Spirit or praise.'"[9] *Tehillah* is used each time the word *praise* appears with the new song. Psalm 22:3: "Yet Thou art holy, O Thou who art enthroned upon the praises [tehillah] of Israel."

Another word for praise is *laud*. *Laud* means to praise (a person or their achievements) highly, especially in a public context.[10] Romans 15:11 says, "And again, Praise the Lord, all ye Gentiles; and *laud* him, all ye people" (emphasis added).

> ...that I may shew forth all thy praise in the gates of the daughter of Zion: I will rejoice in thy salvation.
>
> —Psalm 9:14

> Praise waiteth for thee, O God, in Sion: and unto thee shall the vow be performed.
>
> —Psalm 65:1

If you are a Zion believer, then you are a praiser. David established praise in Zion. David was from a Judah. Jesus is the Lion of Judah. Zion is in Judah, which means praise.

> But God chose the tribe of Judah, the mount Zion which he loved.
>
> —Psalm 78:68

God loves Zion. God loves you. God chooses praise (Judah). You are Zion, and praise is your portion. We rejoice in God's salvation.

Praise is mentioned 150 times in the Book of Psalms (kjv). Many psalms are attributed to David. Zion is the city of David. Zion is the city of praise. Praise includes singing new songs, dancing, shouting, rejoicing, and playing musical instruments.

> Great is the Lord, and greatly to be praised in the city of our God, in the mountain of his holiness.
>
> —Psalm 48:1

God is greatly praised in Zion. God is great in Zion. We declare his greatness. God is highly praised in Zion. High praise is another characteristic of Zion believers. The high praises of God are in our mouths (Ps. 149:6). Some translations render *high praise* as "shouting."

> Cry out and shout, thou inhabitant of Zion: for great is the
> Holy One of Israel in the midst of thee.
>
> —ISAIAH 12:6

The saints are commanded to shout for joy (Ps. 5:11). We clap
our hands and shout for joy with the voice of triumph (Ps. 47:1).
God goes up with a shout (Ps. 47:5). Zion is a place of shouting.

> Rejoice greatly, O daughter of Zion; shout, O daughter of
> Jerusalem: behold, thy King cometh unto thee: he is just, and
> having salvation; lowly, and riding upon an ass, and upon a
> colt the foal of an ass.
>
> —ZECHARIAH 9:9

Singing and shouting are normal for Zion believers. Zion shouts
because of the king. The king's salvation causes this rejoicing. Zion
is commanded to be glad and rejoice with all the heart.

> Sing, O daughter of Zion; shout, O Israel; be glad and rejoice
> with all the heart, O daughter.
>
> —ZEPHANIAH 3:14

Zion loves musical instruments. Zion believers make a joyful
noise. They play upon the high-sounding cymbals (Ps. 150:5).
Zion makes a loud noise (Ps. 98:4).

> Thus all Israel brought up the ark of the covenant of the
> LORD with shouting, and with sound of the cornet, and with
> trumpets, and with cymbals, making a noise with psalteries
> and harps.
>
> —1 CHRONICLES 15:28

The musicians in Zion are commanded to play skillfully with
a loud noise. The singers and players of instruments are in Zion
(Ps. 87:7).

David loved musical instruments. David made musical instruments for the Levites to play (2 Chron. 7:6; 29:26). These musical
instruments were still being played in the days of Nehemiah
(Neh. 12:36)

> Moreover four thousand were porters; and four thousand praised the LORD with the instruments which I made, said David, to praise therewith.
>
> —1 CHRONICLES 23:5

One Hebrew word for *praise* is *zamar*, which means to touch the strings.[11] David was a prophet and a musician who brought together music and the prophetic in Zion. David prophesied upon an instrument. We also prophesy today with instruments of music.

Zion is a place of prophecy and music. Zion believers prophesy. The word of the Lord is in Zion. You are Zion; therefore you are prophetic. You love the music in Zion. Musicians move the hand of the Lord and stir prophets (1 Sam. 10:5; 2 Kings 3:15).

Zion believers are worshipping warriors.

Before Zion became the city of David, it had to be conquered. No one, from Joshua to David, had conquered this fortress. The people of Israel had gone into the land and driven out many inhabitants, but they had not taken the stronghold of Zion.

Zion was a high place, set in the mountains. Its position alone made it difficult to defeat. Anytime you hold a high position, you have a significant advantage over enemy attacks. The Jebusites had built Zion up as an impenetrable fortress, which no one could conquer until David showed up.

It took a certain kind of anointing to take the stronghold. David was a warrior and a worshipper. He had the kind of anointing it takes to press into the presence of the Lord and receive strategy to take over territories for the kingdom. The Bible says David conquered the Jebusites by going up through the gutter of the city (2 Sam. 5:8). Every enemy has a weakness. David discovered the Jebusites' weakness and overtook their city.

I remember years ago we used to sing a song called "We Are Worshipping Warriors." It takes worshipping warriors, a Davidic kind of people, to overtake strongholds. So now Zion belongs to Davidic people, people who are not just ordinary people. These people are worshippers and warriors. They know how to fight and cast out devils. They know how to deal with demons and strongholds, but they also know how to lay their swords down. They know how to bow down and worship God.

Zion is a place of worshippers and warriors. When you get around Zion people, you will find they are people who know how to fight in the spirit. They're not weak people. They know how to bind, and they know how to loose. They know how to cast out. They know how to use their faith. They don't roll over and die when they come under attack. In fact, when Zion people come under attack, the warrior is stirred up on the inside of them, and they don't back down and run. They don't give up and throw in the towel. So when I look for Zion, I look for a people who know how to fight, people who have been through some battles and challenges. They've fought some demons and conquered some Goliaths, bears, and lions. Zion believers are overcomers.

You are Zion. Therefore you are an overcomer. You've overcome witchcraft, control, sickness, disease, poverty, shame, rejection, rebellion, disobedience, lust, and perversion. You have received the victory over so many areas in your life, and that makes you the praiser and worshipper you are today.

When David came into the city after recapturing the ark, his wife Michal looked at him and despised him in her heart (2 Sam. 6:16). She couldn't understand why David was praising and worshipping with such passion. But David had so much to praise God for because David was a man who overcame his enemies. He overcame Saul, the bear, and the lion. He killed Goliath. And David knew each victory came because God was with him. With a heart of deep gratitude David praised God as the source of his victories and deliverance.

Zion believers know how to pray. They know how to rebuke Satan and use their faith and drive out the works of the enemy. In my life, before I learned anything about Zion and worship, the Lord brought me into deliverance and spiritual warfare. I learned about demons and how to cast them out, and I learned how to go through deliverance. I learned how to take people through deliverance. I learned how to wrestle not against flesh and blood but against principalities and powers (Eph. 6:12). God developed in me a warring kind of anointing, and the moment I come under attack, something inside of me rises up; something gets stirred. I realized it is because I'm in Zion that I have become the fighter I am. I'm in the place God chooses—the place He blesses and defends. I am in a place of victory.

When God searched for a place to dwell, He chose the city of David because David had something God liked. David was a worshipper and warrior. Of all the people God could have chosen, He chose David, a man after His own heart. God looks for what I call worshipping warriors—people who know how to fight but also know how to weep. They know how to roar but also know how to bow down. They know how to deal with the powers of hell, but at the same time, they are pliable in His hands. They know how to yield and bend to the will of God. They know how to walk in tenderness, love, and humility. They know how to be strong and bold as a lion but also have the nature of the Lamb. They know how to be vulnerable, soft, and broken in the presence of God. They know how to repent and aren't too proud to ask for forgiveness when they've done something wrong. They can go from fighting to worshipping, from warring to praise. This is what makes up the heart of a Zion believer. This is the place—the heart—in which God wants to dwell. These characteristics defined the heart of David: a heart that followed after God.

David knew he was a champion and warrior, but he also knew how to bow, weep, worship, and cry before the Lord. He knew how to pour out his heart before God. David knew how to stand against the powers of hell, but at the same time, he was a man who was open and honest before God. He told God what his problems were. He told God when he was down. He was a man who had overcome, and the worship David established in Zion demonstrated that.

Zion is a place of musicians and instruments, of singers and dancers. Zion is a place of shouting and celebration. Zion is a place of liberty, joy, victory, revelation, and glory. And most of all, Zion is a place of God's presence.

So ask yourself, Are you Zion? Is your heart a place where God desires to dwell? Is your heart surrendered to praise and worship, shouting, and dancing? Are you abandoned in passionate celebration and adoration of the King? Do you have a heart that will be relentless in driving out the enemy?

It is important to understand God is particular about where He lives. He chooses certain places and will not live just anywhere. It's amazing how we make a choice where we want to live, but then we will think God is supposed to go anywhere. Let me assure you; He will not. God is picky and has made His choice clear about the environment where His holiness will abide. God chooses Zion. He said it would be His dwelling place forever. In other words, from generation to generation to generation He will always choose Zion. He will always look for a people who have the heart of Zion—a heart of worship and a heart of praise—because He inhabits the praises of His people.

The Lord is always searching for you, Zion believer. He desires to make you His habitation. He goes from city to city, state to state, and nation to nation inspecting hearts. He is always looking for Zion. He is always searching for those people who will worship and war. He is always looking for those whom He can choose—those who have chosen to please Him and to desire Him above all else. He will pass over states, cities, and regions. He will go to the uttermost parts of the earth until He finds a Zion heart.

The Bible says, "For the eyes of the LORD run to and fro throughout the whole earth, to shew himself strong in the behalf of them whose heart is perfect toward him" (2 Chron. 16:9).

God has been looking for you, Zion. God chooses to rest in your life forever. As you take on this identity, receiving and walking in the reality of it in every area of your life, you will see victory after victory, breakthrough after breakthrough, and miracle after miracle. You are who God desires. You are not ordinary—you are peculiar. You are the chosen dwelling place of God. Receive this revelation that you are the Zion of God because of Jesus, and worship even now.

DECLARATIONS OF THE WORSHIPPING WARRIOR

I am Zion. God is found in me. God dwells with me and abides in my life. I am ready for breakthroughs I've never had before.

I am Zion, and God has chosen me.

I am Zion. No weapon formed against me shall prosper (Isa. 54:17). Zion knows no defeat. Zion always wins.

I am Zion. Greater is He that is in me than he that is in the world (1 John 4:4).

I will not be defeated.

I will have victory after victory after victory all the days of my life.

I am Zion. I always win.

Wherever I am, Zion is. Zion is here because I'm here.

When I release a shout, when I release a praise, when I dance, or when I release a word, I shatter the strongholds of darkness.

I am Zion. I know who I am. God has given me a new identity. I am not who I used to be.

I am Zion.

Chapter 7

THE BLESSINGS OF ZION (PART 1)—THE GLORY REALM

*Arise [from the depression and prostration in which
circumstances have kept you—rise to a new life]! Shine
(be radiant with the glory of the Lord), for your light has
come, and the glory of the Lord has risen upon you!*
—ISAIAH 60:1, AMPC

I AM BREAKING THE blessings of Zion into two chapters because there is so much I want to share. In this chapter I will introduce and define *glory*. Then in the next chapter I will break down the first part of Isaiah 60, verse by verse, to highlight the blessings and benefits of the glory of God in your life.

I have ministered on the glory realm for years and have been stirred by its revelations. I have seen many believers walk in new realms of fruitfulness as a result of this revelation, and I believe you will too.

The first thing you need to understand is that as a Zion believer you have been called to the glory realm. The glory realm is the realm where God lives. It is the realm of God's dominion, beauty, majesty, splendor, and power. A *realm* is defined as "the region, sphere, or domain within which anything occurs, prevails, or dominates."[1] The kingdom of God is the realm of God's glory.

Glory is a major theme of the Scriptures. God the Father is the Father of glory; the Son is the Lord of glory; and the Holy Spirit is the Spirit of glory (Eph. 1:17; Rom. 6:4; John 1:14; 1 Pet. 4:14). It was always the plan of God for the earth to be filled with His glory (Num. 14:21). Throughout all the ages His church is a glorious church (Eph. 3:21).

The Hebrew word for *glory* is *kabowd*. *Kabowd* means weight, abundance, honor, glory, splendor, wealth, riches, reverence, dignity.[2] The Greek word for *glory* is *doxa*, meaning honor, renown, glory, as especially divine quality, the unspoken manifestation of God, splendor.[3] The Hebrew word for *beauty* is *noam*, meaning splendor or grace.[4] The Hebrew word for *majesty* is *ga'own* meaning high, excellency, of a king or dignitary.[5] Other synonyms for *glory* include *radiant, dazzling, shining,* and *brightness.*[6] God dwells in light that no man can approach (1 Tim. 6:16).

We have been called to glory. We have been called to the kingdom. We can live in the glory realm, and when you do so, it will change your life. Great benefits come from the glory. Nothing compares to this realm. It is above and over every other realm.

Our God is the God of glory. The Lord is the Lord of glory. The Spirit is the Spirit of glory.

God's glory is so many things. Glory is excellence, perfection, and flawlessness. It has no spots, no wrong, and no evil. Because of the beauty of God's holiness and glory, He cannot improve. He has no blemish. He is perfect in all His ways (Ps. 18:30). To touch God is to touch His excellence and perfection. There is nothing higher or greater.

Glory is God's fame and reputation. Our God is above all gods, more famous than all (Ps. 95:3). We declare His fame and glory.

Glory is God's wisdom and honor. His wisdom surpasses all. His understanding is infinite. We honor the God of glory. We bless and speak highly of Him every day. We exalt Him forever.

Glory is God's power and strength. Nothing is impossible to Him. His might is infinite. His power is great.

Glory is God's riches and wealth. Riches belong to Him. The gold and silver are His (Hag. 2:8). His glory brings abundance and prosperity.

God's glory is His magnificence and majesty. Majesty is splendor, excellence, highness, and royalty.[7]

God's glory is His light. God is light, and in Him is no darkness (John 1:5). His light shines, and He illuminates with His glory.

THE LIGHT OF GLORY

Arise, shine; for thy light is come, and the glory of the LORD is risen upon thee.

—ISAIAH 60:1

Isaiah chapter 60 describes Zion's restoration, but the whole prophecy is also one of restoration for Zion through Christ the Messiah. Isaiah is prophesying about the glory of Zion in this amazing chapter that describes the blessings that belong to Zion. God's promises to Zion are the most amazing of any made to any city and people in history.

The first word spoken in the prophecy is *arise*. When Isaiah wrote this, Zion (Israel) had been judged because of its covenantal violations and had gone into captivity in Babylon. This was a call to them to get up from a low place and to arise from the dust (Isa. 52:2).

But Zion was in mourning and under judgment for breaking the covenant and shedding the blood of the prophets. Israel wept by the rivers of Babylon (Ps. 137:1). They could not sing the songs of Zion in a strange land (Ps. 137:3–4).

The prophets had prophesied the time of judgment (the Lamentations of Jeremiah mention Zion fifteen times), but then they prophesied a coming glory. This coming glory upon Zion would bring salvation and blessing to the world. God would turn Zion's captivity and redeem the people through Christ. God's mercy on Zion brought restoration.

When the LORD turned again the captivity of Zion, we were like them that dream.

—PSALM 126:1

Zion is first told to arise. Synonyms for *arise* are *come to light*, *become apparent*, *appear*, *emerge*, *surface*, and *spring up*.[8] God wants Zion to come forth out of darkness and obscurity. This arising would make Zion visible to the world.

Zion is then told to shine. Synonyms for *shine* include *glow*, *radiate*, *beam*, and *sparkle*.[9] Zion shines in the darkness. This is a picture of light and illumination. This shining would be the result of glory. This is why I believe Isaiah 60 is talking about the glory of Zion.

Zion is glorious. Zion carries the glory of God. The prophecy of Isaiah gives us a picture of what happens when glory comes upon a people. The blessings of glory are amazing and far-reaching.

These blessings and benefits will also come upon your life because you are Zion. You can arise. You can shine. The glory of God is shining on *you*.

> For, behold, the darkness shall cover the earth, and gross darkness the people: but the LORD shall arise upon thee, and his glory shall be seen upon thee.
>
> —ISAIAH 60:2

Glory is light. Glory is God's brightness. God shines from between the cherubim (Ps. 80:1), and His face shines upon us. This is a picture of God's blessing and favor. God shines out of Zion (Ps. 50:2). The glory makes you attractive. It causes you to stand out.

Glory is light and illumination. Because God is light, glory is God's essence, which is light. Light produces clarity, sight, and vision. The glory of God will bring insight, wisdom, knowledge, and understanding into your life. It brings revelation, so we understand the hidden things, the mysteries of God.

Light is a manifestation of glory. Glory is brightness, shining, and brilliance. Jesus is the Light. Jesus is the Light of our lives. Jesus is the glory and light of God inside of us. His glory shines in the darkness. Those in darkness are attracted and come to the light.

Darkness is ignorance, obscurity, and shadiness. Darkness is a lack of wisdom. People grope in darkness. Darkness is a lack of direction and purpose. But glory overwhelms darkness and drives it out.

> The sun shall be no more thy light by day; neither for brightness shall the moon give light unto thee: but the LORD shall be unto thee an everlasting light, and thy God thy glory. Thy sun shall no more go down; neither shall thy moon withdraw itself: for the LORD shall be thine everlasting light, and the days of thy mourning shall be ended.
>
> —ISAIAH 60:19–20

You are Zion. You are a light and shine in the darkness. You reflect the light of heaven, and the light of Zion fills the earth through you.

GLORY IS BEAUTIFUL

Glory is also God's beauty and splendor. No one or nothing is more beautiful than God. The glory realm is a realm of sapphire, emerald, topaz, ruby, and diamond.[10] Glory shines. Glory is brilliance, greater than precious stones.

The beauty of glory is what makes God attractive to us. His glory draws us to Him. His glory amazes and dazzles. The nations are drawn to the beauty of God's glory. All are drawn to behold, worship, and bow down.

Zion is called the perfection of God's beauty (Ps. 50:2), and as glory comes into your life, you will be made beautiful. You will be strengthened. You will be made stable.

The trees of Lebanon are another picture of glory:

> The glory of Lebanon shall come unto thee, the fir tree, the pine tree, and the box together, to beautify the place of my sanctuary; and I will make the place of my feet glorious.
>
> —ISAIAH 60:13

Lebanon is known for its beauty and its trees. Trees represent strength, stature, and height. Trees are stable and strong:

> It [the desert] shall blossom abundantly, and rejoice even with joy and singing: the glory of Lebanon shall be given unto it, the excellency of Carmel and Sharon, they shall see the glory of the LORD, and the excellency of our God.
> —ISAIAH 35:2

The glory of Lebanon is even given to the desert of Zion. The beauty, splendor, and majesty of God's glory come into your life. Even though you were like a desert, the glory of God makes you beautiful and majestic.

The glory also causes you to see the excellence and beauty of God in everything around you. It will cause you to see through eyes of beauty. It will cause you not to get discouraged and bitter when you see flaws in others and in yourself.

You can get discouraged if you look at imperfection, and hell tries to get you to do that to release desolation in your life. That's why Zion believers fix their eyes on God. They break away from false images, destructive lies, and thought barriers of limitation.

God has beauty for you. The blessing coming to you brings strength, life, and beauty. You are God's canvas, and He is painting a masterpiece in your life. You will be a living reflection of His creativity and splendor.

Lebanon is also known for its majestic cedars. They represent growth, abundance, and blessing. Other Bible versions translate Isaiah 35:2 as majestic, beautiful, or green. The Contemporary English Version of the Bible says, "They will be as majestic as Mount Lebanon." The Easy-to-Read Version says, "It will be as beautiful as the forest of Lebanon." The New Living Translation says, "The deserts will become as green as the mountains of Lebanon."

We grow like the cedars in Lebanon (Ps. 92:12). These trees are filled with sap (moisture) (Ps. 104:16); God plants the cedars in the wilderness (Isa. 41:19). These scriptures picture cedars as depictions of exaltation and blessing. Even Solomon spoke of the cedar (1 Kings 4:33). Therefore the cedar is a picture of wisdom. The cedar is also a picture of cleansing and freshness (Lev. 14:4).

The cedars of Lebanon are known for their height. The glory causes us to grow, which brings height and stature to our lives. We are not shrubs; we are cedars. The cedar is also a picture of excellence (Song of Sol. 5:15). Cedars provide strength to the house (Song of Sol. 1:17).

Begin to believe and confess the glory of Lebanon is coming toward you.

GLORY IS EXCELLENT AND JOYOUS

The glory delivers us from rejection, and cause us to become an eternal excellency.

> Whereas thou has been forsaken and hated, so that no man went through thee, I will make thee an eternal excellency, a joy of many generations.
>
> —ISAIAH 60:15

Excellency is about having outstanding or valuable quality. Excellence is the highest. When you are excellent, you surpass all others. Excellence can be used in reference to virtue, dignity, worth, or superiority. Zion is an eternal excellence. You are Zion. You have excellence.

Different Bible translations use other words for *excellence*: *swelling, rising, superabundance, honor, beauty, majesty, uplifted,* and *elevation.* The Greek word for *excellence* is *huperoché* meaning "prominence, preeminent (superior)," and "a projection...as a mountain peak."[11] Zion excels. You are Zion. You will excel.

God's glory is excellent (2 Pet. 1:17). Glory is supreme. Glory is majestic. God's glory brings excellence to your life.

This excellence is coupled with joy. Zion is the joy of many generations, and the joy of the Lord is our strength (Neh. 8:10). We have the oil of joy (Isa. 61:3). We obtain joy and gladness (Isa.

35:10). We possess the double portion or honor (Isa. 61:7). We shout for joy (Ps. 5:11). In God's presence is the fullness of joy (Ps. 16:11). We offer the sacrifices of joy (Ps. 27:6).

Zion is called the joy of the whole earth (Ps. 48:2). Zion is the city of joy. Zion people are people of joy. The kingdom of God is joy (Rom. 14:17). The people who know the joyful sound are blessed (Ps. 89:15). We are joyful in glory (Ps. 149:5).

GLORY IS RICH AND BOUNTIFUL

> Thou shalt also suck the milk of the Gentiles, and shalt suck
> the breast of kings: and thou shalt know that I the LORD am
> thy Saviour and thy Redeemer, the mighty One of Jacob.
> —ISAIAH 60:16

Milk represents nourishment and fatness. Milk represents richness (butter). Babes are nourished from their mother's milk. Milk produces strength and growth. Zion sucks the breasts (riches) of kings. Zion receives the blessings of the breasts (Gen. 49:25).

One of my favorite Hebrew terms is El Shaddai. God revealed Himself to Abraham as El Shaddai—the Almighty God (Gen. 17:1). The Hebrew word *shaddai* comes from two root words. The first is a root word meaning powerful. The second root means breast or nourisher and sustainer. The Old Testament uses El Shaddai forty-eight times.[12]

The hills flow with milk in the kingdom (Joel 3:18). This is another picture of abundance and blessing. Because you are Zion, you are nourished. You drink plentifully. You are sustained by God.

> ...that ye may suck, and be satisfied with the breasts of her
> consolations; that ye may milk out, and be delighted with
> the abundance of her glory.
> —ISAIAH 66:11

Milk is also a picture of glory (riches, abundance, satisfaction, delight, bounty) as well as consolation and comfort. The Amplified Bible calls this a "bountiful" bosom. Zion is a place of bountiful blessings, and you are Zion. You enjoy bountiful blessings. You have abundance and satisfaction.

GLORY DELIVERS US INTO PEACE AND PROSPERITY

Shalom is another of my favorite Hebrew words. It is usually translated "peace," but it has a much deeper and richer meaning. *Shalom* means "safe, i.e. (figuratively) well, happy, friendly; also (abstractly) welfare, i.e. health, prosperity, peace…(good) health, prosperity, rest, safety, salute, welfare, well."[13]

The Amplified Bible says, "And [instead of the tyranny of the present] I will appoint peace as your officers" (Isa. 60:17). You will not have tyrants ruling over you. You will not be oppressed. Peace (shalom) will be your ruler.

Peace brings prosperity. Solomon's name is from the root word *shalom.*[14] Solomon's kingdom was one of peace and prosperity. Solomon was a type of Christ and His kingdom. Zion is a place of peace, property, and wisdom. You are Zion. You are filled with peace. You are prosperous.

God extends peace to Zion like a river (Isa. 66:12). The glory of the nations come to Zion like a flowing stream. Peace flows in your life. There is a river that brings a constant flow of shalom to you. Isaiah 66:12 in the Good News Translation says, "I will bring you lasting prosperity; the wealth of the nations will flow to you like a river that never goes dry." The river of God in your life is a river of peace and prosperity.

Isaiah 60:17 in the Amplified Bible says, "…righteousness your rulers." The glory delivers us from unrighteousness rulers. We do not live under despots and tyrants.

Righteousness is justice. Justice becomes your ruler. In other words, you will not live under unjust leaders and rulers. You are Zion. You are free from wicked and unjust rulers. You will not be subject to cruelty and mistreatment. This is another level of peace the Zion believer can live in. (See Proverbs 29:2; 1 Timothy 2:1–2.)

Zion is a place of the rule and reign of Christ. This is the kingdom of God. Zion is subject to Christ's rule. Righteousness is the scepter of the kingdom (Heb. 1:8). You are Zion. You live under the rule of righteousness.

This peace brings two other blessings:

Violence, wasting, and destruction will be removed from your life.

> Violence shall no more be heard in thy land, wasting nor destruction within thy borders; but thou shalt call thy walls Salvation, and thy gates Praise.
>
> —ISAIAH 60:18

Violence, wasting, and destruction are the enemies of peace and prosperity. No one wants to live in a land plagued by violence. Violence produces fear, anger, bitterness, and hatred.

Satan loves violence and wasting, but you are Zion. You are redeemed from deceit and violence (Ps. 72:14). You are delivered from the violent man (Ps. 18:48). You are redeemed from destruction (Ps. 103:4). The destroyers that make haste depart from you (Isa. 49:17). Your destroyers and plunderers are leaving and going.

You are Zion. You will not be plundered. You are not a spoil. You will not be devoured by the enemy. You are free from violence. Your borders are filled with peace and the finest of the wheat (Ps. 147:14).

Walls of salvation and gates of praise will be erected in your life.

You are Zion, and your walls are salvation. The Greek word for *salvation* is *sozo*, and it means, "to save, keep safe and sound, to rescue from danger or destruction; to save a suffering one (from perishing), i.e. one suffering from disease, to make well, heal, restore to health; to preserve one who is in danger of destruction, to save or rescue; to deliver from the penalties of the Messianic judgment; to save from the evils which obstruct the reception of the Messianic deliverance."[15]

Walls protect from outside invasion. You are Zion, and you are protected. You have walls. You are not defenseless. Salvation protects us from evil.

Salvation means deliverance.[16] Since Zion is delivered and protected, it means you are delivered from the plans and attacks of hell. You have been delivered from the power of darkness (Col. 1:13).

Within the walls of Zion are the gates of praise. Gates represent access. Isaiah 60:18 says, "Salvation will surround you like city walls, and praise will be on the lips of all who enter there" (NLT). Those who come to Zion come with praise. You enter the city through praise. Praise gives you access. We enter His gates with thanksgiving and His courts with praise (Ps. 100:4).

Praise opens your gates to the blessings of God. Remember, your gates are open continuously. We are called to praise God continually (Ps. 34:1).

INHERIT THE LAND, AND GLORIFY GOD

Thy people also shall be all righteous: they shall inherit the land for ever, the branch of my planting, the work of my hands, that I may be glorified.

—ISAIAH 60:21

The land God promised is the place of promise, blessing, inheritance, the kingdom, abundance, shalom, prosperity, water, refreshing, might, power, wealth, overflow, life, growth, glory, presence, favor, salvation, deliverance, safety, protection, praise, and rest. You enter this land by patience, waiting, trust, and faith.

Psalm 37 is the psalm that talks about inheriting the land. The meek inherit the earth. The righteous inherit the land. Those who trust in the Lord inherit the land (Ps. 37:3). Those who wait on the Lord and keep His way are exalted to inherit the land (Ps. 37:34).

In the Old Testament the land meant everything to the Hebrews. Each tribe, except Levi, had a portion. God promised the land to Abraham and his seed. They were told to go in and drive the enemy out. To live in the land in peace was the result of God's blessing, and when they came under judgment, they were removed from the land.

Jesus was the true seed of Abraham. We are Abraham's seed through Christ (Gal. 3:29). We inherit the land through Christ. We enter the blessing through faith in Christ.

The land is a picture of Christ and the kingdom, a land flowing with milk and honey. Because you are Zion, you inherit the land. You inherit the promises of God.

We are planted in the land. We are rooted and grounded in the faith. God is glorified by us living in the land.

CONFESSIONS FROM PSALM 37

I will not fret because of evildoers.

I will trust in the Lord and do good.

I will dwell in the land and be fed.

I delight myself in the Lord.

I receive the desires of my heart.

I commit my way unto the Lord.

My righteousness will come forth as the light, and my judgment as the noonday.

I rest in the Lord and wait patiently for Him.

I cease from anger, and I forsake wrath.

I will inherit the land.

I will walk in meekness and inherit the land.

I will delight myself in the abundance of peace.

The Lord upholds me.

My inheritance is forever.

I will not be ashamed in the evil time.

I will be satisfied in the days of famine.

I am blessed, and I inherit the land.

My steps are ordered by the Lord. The Lord upholds me with His hand.

I am merciful, and I lend, and my seed is blessed.

I depart from evil, I do good, and I will dwell in the land forevermore.

I inherit the land and dwell in it forever.

The law of God is in my heart, and my steps will not slide.

I wait on the Lord and keep His way.

I will be exalted to inherit the land.

I will see when the wicked are cut off.

I am perfect and upright, and my end is peace.

My salvation is of the Lord, and He is my strength in the time of trouble.

The Lord will help me and deliver me from the wicked and save me because I trust in Him.

Chapter 8

THE BLESSINGS OF ZION (PART 2)—YOU CAN'T STAY SMALL

Enlarge the place of thy tent, and let them stretch forth
the curtains of thine habitations: spare not, lengthen thy
cords, and strengthen thy stakes; for thou shalt break forth
on the right hand and on the left; and thy seed shall inherit
the Gentiles, and make the desolate cities to be inhabited.
—ISAIAH 54:2–3

THE GLORY OF God breaks limitations off your life so that you can increase and enlarge. Zion is the enlarged tent of Israel. If you are a Zion believer, you need to make room!

It was toward the end of 2017 when God spoke this word to me: "You can't stay small." I had been meditating on Isaiah chapter 60 for many years by then, but He began to take me deeper into what His thoughts were for His people as they grow in their understanding of what His glory means in their lives.

Let me say this: there is nothing wrong with starting small. Despise not the day of small beginnings (Zech. 4:10), because often when we start small, we are starting in a place of humility. We are just learning. We are new or novice, somewhat naïve, and even more so, we are teachable, and God will bless us. However, we should expect that as we remain faithful, He will increase us. We should not resist the effect that God's glory has on our lives. When His glory comes, we can expect to expand and grow. There are consequences to our enjoying life in God when we resist the expansion that comes with His glory.

Brian Houston, the founding pastor of Hillsong Church, says this: "Smallness inside a man (smallness of thinking and spirit) will shrink his world, shrink his children, and shrink his potential."[1] God doesn't want us to stay small. It is OK to start small. Just don't stay small. So if you feel as if you have been in a small place—insignificant, overlooked, ignored, no power, no influence, no platform, no voice, or no finances—know it is God's will that you increase, expand, and enlarge.

One way to get increase in your life is the glory of God. When God's glory comes upon a city, nation, community, church, or individual—when an individual accesses God's presence, God's glory, God's Shekinah—there is no limit to the growth and expansion God will bring. So much happens when you encounter the glory of God, and one way to do this is through worship. Worship is the doorway into the glory realm.

As we have learned, Zion believers are worshippers. Zion worship should be prophetic, and it should bring the presence of God. When you get into the glory realm, you experience healing, miracles, prophetic words, breakthroughs, salvations, deliverance, and more. Zion believers love the glory of God because it is a realm where nothing is impossible.

Not many churches press into the glory realm, and they leave much to be desired in terms of the supernatural. It may be because of time constraints that they don't press in or because they simply don't desire it. Two fast songs and two slow songs on a Sunday, and they just move on. But sometimes it takes time for that realm to open up. Sometimes it opens up quickly. Other times you have to spend time pressing in by faith and flowing with the Spirit of God.

The glory of the Lord must be something we desire. In Psalm 27:4 David said, "One thing I have desired of the LORD, that will I seek: that I may dwell in the house of the LORD all the days of my life, to behold the beauty of the LORD, and to inquire in His temple." As we have discovered, the beauty of the Lord is His glory, which is one of the first characteristics that cause you to be enlarged. The beauty of the glory of the Lord will draw people to you, causing you to increase.

In this chapter we will move through Isaiah 60 and learn how the glory of Zion comes into your life and promotes, increases, and expands you. Zion believers cannot stay small in the glory. The glory of the Lord enlarges and increases the capacity of the Zion believer's heart and mind, preparing them for expansion.

THE GLORY WILL DRAW PEOPLE TO YOU

> Arise, shine; for your light has come! And the glory of the LORD is risen upon you. For behold, the darkness shall cover the earth, and deep darkness the people; but the LORD will arise over you, and His glory will be seen upon you.
>
> —ISAIAH 60:1–2

When the glory comes, it causes you to arise. The word *arise* means to increase, to come to a higher elevation, to be promoted.[2] The light of glory will cause you to shine and be attractive to influential people. They will be attracted to your light; the nations, the Gentiles will come to your light. Kings, rulers, chiefs, CEOs, those with authority, power, influence will come like a magnet to the glory emitted from your life.

You will receive favor, sponsorship, partnerships, glorious projects, help, and continued blessings. People will come into your life when you arise and shine because you carry the glory of God. You will not have to recruit anyone. The glory will bring them.

Verse 3 says, "And the Gentiles shall come to thy light, and kings to the brightness of thy rising." The Gentiles were those outside of Israel. They were the people who were without covenant, the uncircumcised. They would come to Zion's light.

Kings would come. Kings represent influential people. Kings are those with authority and following. The queen of Sheba was attracted to the glory and wisdom in Solomon's kingdom. She came from the uttermost part of the earth to hear Solomon's wisdom (1 Kings 10:1; Matt. 12:42).

Jesus is greater than Solomon. Jesus lives inside the believer. People come to the glory upon you and in you through Christ. The Gentiles represent the nations. God loves all nations and desires them to come to the light. Zion had to arise and shine. This is what happens when you arise and shine. Those in darkness see and come to you. This is your calling. You are Zion.

THE GLORY INCREASES THE GATHERING ANOINTING

> Lift up thine eyes round about, and see: all they gather themselves together, they come to thee: thy sons shall come from far, and thy daughters shall be nursed at thy side.
>
> —ISAIAH 60:4

The glory causes people to gather, to come to you. There is a gathering anointing that comes when the glory comes. This applies to your life and to churches who center the ark—the presence of God, the glory of God—in the midst of their service and ministry. This is about developing a culture of glory, honor, praise, worship, majesty, splendor, and the light of God in your life, ministry, business, or whatever God has called you to do.

It will be the light of God's glory that will cause people to gather around you. This is a picture of influence and power. People gather because they see the glory. They come to the glory to be saved and delivered. They do not come empty-handed. They come ready to give and present themselves to Zion.

The ability to gather people is a sign of God's anointing and gifting. Multitudes gathered to Christ from all over Galilee. The sick gathered to be healed. The demonized gathered to be delivered. The hopeless gathered to receive hope. The ignorant gathered to be taught. People gathered to hear the preaching of the gospel, and they gathered to Jesus received miracles.

In the second half of verse 4 we see the glory brings sons and daughters, which for your life may mean spiritual sons and daughters, people who need mentorship and training for living out their purposes. Because the glory of God is also the wisdom of God, people will be drawn to your wisdom when the glory of God comes upon your life.

THE GLORY WILL ENLARGE THE CAPACITY OF YOUR HEART

> Then thou shalt see, and flow together, and thine heart shall fear, and be enlarged; because the abundance of the sea shall be converted unto thee, the forces of the Gentiles shall come unto thee.
>
> —ISAIAH 60:5

When the glory comes, it enlarges your heart. This verse is where the revelation for "You can't stay small" comes from. The Complete Jewish Bible translates "and be enlarged" as "throb and swell with delight." Other translations say your heart will be thrilled, tremble with excitement, be excited, and overflow. In other words, so much will happen so fast until your heart leaps for joy.

This prophecy speaks of abundance coming to Zion. The forces (*chayil*) of the nations come to Zion. *Chayil* is such a powerful Hebrew word. *Chayil* is often translated as "wealth." I will explain it more as it relates to your Zion identity in chapter 10.

The glory of Zion enlarges your faith, your mind, your vision, and your capacity. With all that comes the glory of God, and you must have the room to receive it and embrace it. Your ability to dream and how you think need to be enlarged to handle the increase and expansion that comes from the glory. The verse says, "The abundance of the sea shall be converted unto thee, the forces [or wealth] of the Gentiles shall come unto thee." The word *forces* in the Hebrew is *chayil* (wealth).[3] So abundance and wealth come into your life, and your heart is enlarged to receive it because of the glory.

The word *heart* in verse 5 is synonymous with mind, understanding, will, and thinking.[4]

THE GLORY WILL DRAW MULTITUDES

In verse 6 it says, "The multitude of camels shall cover thee, the dromedaries of Midian and Ephah; all they from Sheba shall come: they shall bring gold and incense; and they shall shew forth the praises of the LORD." Notice the phrase "the multitude of camels." The "multitude" represents increase, and the "multitude of camels" represents a caravan.

I preached a message one time called "Your Camels Are Coming." A caravan of camels in the ancient Middle East represented wealth, prosperity, and gifts. Do you recall how the queen of Sheba came to Solomon with caravans of wealth, and how she brought him spices and other precious gifts? Sheba is another picture of wealth coming to Zion from afar. The queen of Sheba came from the utmost of the earth to commune with Solomon (Luke 11:31; Matt. 12:42). She came with a very great train of spices and valuables to give to Solomon (1 Kings 10:2).

Many believe Sheba came from Ethiopia. She represents people coming from afar to praise the Lord in Zion. Dromedaries are camels. Camels are another symbol of blessing. Camels represent a caravan. Caravans are used in trading and represent wealth and prosperity. Those who are sought out will receive caravans of blessings. Say it out loud: "I don't want a bucket of blessing. I don't want a spoonful of blessing. I want the camels! I want the overflow."

> Your country will be covered with caravans of young camels from Midian and Ephah. The people of Sheba will bring gold and spices in praise of me, the LORD.
>
> —ISAIAH 60:6, CEV

This idea of multitude or caravan of camels covering you has to do with the wealth and abundance that comes into your life as a result of the glory.

Another word that speaks of increase is found in verse 7, where it says, "All the flocks of Kedar shall be gathered together unto thee." Flocks can represent sheep, churches, or church members. God wants to enlarge our churches. Churches can and should grow and experience multiplication. When the glory of God hits a church, it will bring flocks. It will bring herds.

THE GLORY WILL CAUSE BLESSINGS AND PROSPERITY TO COME INTO YOUR LIFE

It doesn't take long for blessings to arrive when glory comes. Blessings will fly your way.

> Who are these that fly as a cloud, and as the doves to their windows?
>
> —Isaiah 60:8

This is a picture of blessings coming quickly. Glory speeds up the process. Glory cause the right people to move quickly in your direction.

I love the *Message* paraphrase of Amos 9:13–15, as it connects to this glory benefit:

> "Yes indeed, it won't be long now." God's Decree.

> "Things are going to happen so fast your head will swim, one thing fast on the heels of the other. You won't be able to keep up. Everything will be happening at once—and everywhere you look, blessings! Blessings like wine pouring off the mountains and hills. I'll make everything right again for my people Israel."

Prosperity (silver and gold) will also begin to come into your life. Isaiah 60:9 says,

> Surely the isles shall wait for me, and the ships of Tarshish first, to bring thy sons from far, their silver and their gold with them, unto the name of the LORD thy God, and to the Holy One of Israel, because he hath glorified thee.

The glory always brings prosperity. The gold and silver belong to God (Hag. 2:8). God fills the house with His glory.

THE GLORY WILL REBUILD YOUR WALLS

And the sons of strangers shall build up thy walls, and their kings shall minister unto thee: for in my wrath I smote thee, but in my favour have I had mercy on thee.
—ISAIAH 60:10

This is a picture of restoration where there had been desolation and destruction. After the Babylonian captivity Nehemiah returned to repair and rebuild the walls of Jerusalem, and people gathered to help him. The glory brings people into your life to rebuild your walls.

Zion's walls are rebuilt. You are rebuilt through the ministry of those God sends. The broken places in your life are restored. Zion believers are restored believers. Zion is strong. Zion is protected. Zion is a city with walls (Rev. 21:17–18)

In Revelation the wall of the holy city is made of jasper. According to *Easton's Bible Dictionary*, jasper is from the Hebrew word *yashpheh*, which means "glittering."[5] It is "a gem of various colours, one of the twelve inserted in the high priest's breastplate (Exodus 28:20). It is named in the building of the New Jerusalem (Revelation 21:18; Revelation 21:19). It was 'most precious,' 'clear as crystal' (21:11). It was emblematic of the glory of God (4:3)."[6]

In other words, our walls are glorious and beautiful. Our walls are precious and valuable. Our walls are glittering and shining. This is the beauty and glory of Zion.

Our walls are also like fire:

For I, saith the LORD, will be unto her *a wall of fire round about*, and will be the glory in the midst of her.
—ZECHARIAH 2:5, EMPHASIS ADDED

Here the prophet Zechariah mentions a wall of fire. Fire is another picture of glory and protection. The International

Standard Version of the Bible says, "...an encircling rampart of fire." The Voice translation says, "Instead of a wall of stone, I will be a wall of fire."

THE GLORY WILL OPEN YOUR LIFE TO MULTIPLE BLESSINGS

When the Hebrews were taken into captivity, Jerusalem's gates were destroyed and burned with fire (Neh. 1:3). The gates were desolate (Lam. 1:4). Her gates were sunk in the ground (Lam. 2:9). But Nehemiah came and restored the gates. The gates of Zion are now beautiful and strong. You are Zion. You have strong and beautiful gates.

> Therefore thy gates shall be open continually; they shall not
> be shut day nor night; that men may bring unto thee the
> forces of the Gentiles, and that their kings may be brought.
> —ISAIAH 60:11

Zion's gates are open continually. Open gates represent access. You could not enter a city unless the gates were open. Multiple blessings have access to your life.

As I mentioned earlier (and will continue to discuss in future chapters), "forces" is the Hebrew word *chayil*. *Chayil* means wealth and riches. Most translations use the word *wealth*. Wealth comes to Zion. You are Zion. Wealth comes to you.

Zion, the hill of God, is showered with blessings. Showers represent an abundance, an outpouring, a downpour. Zion is blessed. And because you are Zion, you are the recipient of multiple blessings. Heaven will rain blessings upon your life:

> And I will make them and the places round about my hill
> a blessing; and I will cause the shower to come down in his
> season; there shall be showers of blessing.
> —EZEKIEL 34:26

The Amplified Bible translates this as "There will be [abundant] showers of blessing (divine favor)." Zion believers live under an open heaven.

THE GLORY WILL CAUSE YOU TO BE LIFTED ABOVE THOSE WHO HAVE AFFLICTED YOU

> For the nation and kingdom that will not serve thee shall perish; yea, those nations shall be utterly wasted.... The sons also of them that afflicted thee shall come bending unto thee; and all they that despised thee shall bow themselves down at the soles of thy feet; and they shall call thee; The city of the LORD, The Zion of the Holy One of Israel.
>
> —Isaiah 60:12, 14

God commands people to come and bless Zion. Those who rebel are judged. What a sobering word. The nations have no choice. This is God's command. You are Zion. God has commanded people to bless you.

For those who have afflicted Zion, the tables are turned when the glory comes. Those who afflicted Zion would come and submit. They would no longer afflict. Affliction and oppression are no longer Zion's portion. Zion now has the prominence and authority; Zion is now ruling.

Because you are Zion, you are no longer under affliction. You are now in a new position of power and authority. You are now over your enemies. Isaiah 54:11 says, "O thou afflicted, tossed with tempest, and not comforted, behold, I will lay thy stones with fair colours, and lay thy foundations with sapphires."

THE GLORY WILL UPGRADE YOU

> For brass I will bring gold, and for iron I will bring silver, and for wood brass, and for stones iron: I will also make thy officers peace, and thine exactors righteousness.
>
> —Isaiah 60:17

The glory brings a new level of prosperity. There is an upgrade in the glory. *Upgrade* means "to improve the quality or usefulness of something, or to raise something or someone to a higher position or rank."[7]

We go from brass to gold. We go from iron to silver. We go from wood to brass, and from stones to iron. There is an increase in value when the glory comes. There is an increase in wealth and prosperity.

THE GLORY WILL USHER YOU INTO THE THOUSANDS REALM

Isaiah 60:22 is my favorite scripture on this topic: "A little one shall become a thousand, and a small one a strong nation: I the LORD will hasten it in his time."

The number thousand represents increase as well. I wrote a small book on the topic of thousands that breaks down how God multiplies, increases, and blesses His people. These are the benefits of glory. The blessings of the glory—multitudes, blessing, abundance, enlargement, camels, flocks, herds, increase, thousands—they all come as a result of the glory.

THE GLORY REALM MEETS THE MEGA REALM

And the city lieth foursquare, and the length is as large as the breadth: and he measured the city with the reed, twelve thousand furlongs. The length and the breadth and the height of it are equal.

—REVELATION 21:16

Realizing you are born of Zion and Zion is birthed in you, you should understand the expanse of heavenly Zion is symbolic of the expanse God wants to stretch your heart. Just reading about the immense size of the New Jerusalem is staggering. In Revelation 21:15–16 the angel measures the city with a golden rod or reed and records it as 12,000 stadia by 12,000 stadia at the base, and 12,000 stadia high. A stadia, which is also called a furlong in some translations, is usually considered to be 185 meters or 607 feet, so the base has dimensions of about 2220 kilometers by 2220 kilometers, or 1380 miles by 1380 miles.[8] The Amplified Bible says, "The city is laid out as a square, its length being the same as its width; and he measured the city with his rod—twelve thousand stadia (about 1,400 miles); its length and width and height are equal" (v. 16).

This is no ordinary city. This is a mega city. It has room for multitudes from generation to generation. Zion breaks forth on the right hand and on the left (Isa. 54:3). You are Zion. You are mega.

Mega is from the Greek word *megas,* meaning great, in particular of space and its dimensions as respects mass and weight, large, spacious, long stature and age, numerous, abundant, eminent for ability, virtue, authority, power; things esteemed highly for their importance, of great weight, a thing highly esteemed for its excellence, splendid, prepared on a grand scale, stately, of God's preeminent blessings.[9]

Zion is large enough to receive the forces (chayil) of the nations. The gates are always open. Multitudes come. Abundance comes. The city of God is the largest; no earthly city can compare. The glory realm is the mega realm. Zion is the city of glory, the city of the mega.

As a Zion believer, the glory of the Lord opens up the mega realm of God for you. The scale of what God will do in your life can hardly be measured. Get ready to "enlarge the place of thy tent, and let them stretch forth the curtains of thine habitations" (Isa. 54:2).

HUNGER FOR THE GLORY; INCREASE WILL COME

When you hunger and hunger for the glory, and get into the glory realm—especially through worship—and you worship until the glory comes, the exponential increase of God will be available to you. When you become part of the glory, worship, splendor, and God's majesty, such an enlargement of your vision and your heart will come. This exposure to the glory and power of God will bring such blessing and increase. You cannot stay the same when the glory of God invades your life.

God brings you into a large place because of His glory on the ark around which you center your life. As a Zion believer you choose what God chooses, you have a heart after God, you love to worship, and you love to serve in the courts of the King of kings. Glory will come into your life as a result. You cannot stay small when the glory of God hits your life.

I mentioned these verses in Isaiah 60 throughout this book (and will continue preaching and writing on them as long as the Lord gives me revelation) because I believe they are so important. And I want to challenge you to claim these particular verses as you move into a new downpour of the glory of God in your life. Meditate on them. Believe them. Confess them. Desire the glory of God and to walk in the glory realm, to worship there, and to live there. When you do, God will give you the desires of your heart. Your desires to be an influence in the kingdom, to expand the kingdom, and to see multitudes come into the kingdom will be granted. God will exalt and honor you and make your name great, just as He promised Abraham. You can't stay small. Increase is coming!

CONFESSIONS FOR ENLARGEMENT AND INCREASE

When the glory hits my life,

My faith won't stay small.

My vision won't stay small.

My finances won't stay small.

My influence won't stay small.

My platform won't stay small.

My ideas won't stay small.

My creativity won't stay small.

My strength won't stay small.

My business won't stay small.

My favor can't stay small.

Though my beginning was small, my latter will greatly increase (Job 8:7).

My little will become like a thousand, and my small will become like a strong nation. The Lord will hasten it in His time (Isa. 60:22).

Lord, bless me and enlarge my coast. Let Your right hand be with me. Keep me from evil (1 Chron. 4:10).

The Lord shall increase me more and more, me and my children (Ps. 115:14).

The Lord God of my fathers will make me a thousand times so many more than I am. He will bless me, as He has promised me (Deut. 1:11).

I will enlarge the place of my tent and stretch forth the curtains of my habitations. I will lengthen my cords and strengthen my stakes. I will break forth on the right hand and on the left, and my seed will inherit the nations and inhabit the desolate cities (Isa. 54:1–3).

God brought me forth into a large place. He delivered me because He delighted in me (Ps. 18:19).

God has set my feet in a large room (Ps. 31:8).

I am righteous and flourish like the palm tree. I will grow like a cedar in Lebanon (Ps. 92:12).

I called upon the Lord in distress: the Lord answered me and set me in a large place (Ps. 118:5).

My gift makes room for me and brings me before great men (Prov. 18:16).

I am a fruitful bough, even a fruitful bough by a well. My branches run over the wall (Gen. 49:22).

Chapter 9

THE WEIGHT OF GLORY

For our light affliction, which is but for a moment, worketh
for us a far more exceeding and eternal weight of glory.
—2 CORINTHIANS 4:17

THE GLORY OF Zion is weighty, and as one who has the heart of Zion, you carry the glory, which makes you weighty in the spirit. The glory of God laid upon your life has value and weight.

The Hebrew word for *glory* is *kabod*, meaning "heaviness" or "weight."[1] This is a symbol of prosperity and wealth. The value of gold and silver is determined by weight. Gold and silver are also connected to glory, as we learn from reading Isaiah 60 when it mentions "forces." The word *forces*, as we've discussed, is *chayil*, which also means wealth.

According to the Holman dictionary, *kabod* is "the weighty importance and shining majesty that accompany God's presence. The basic meaning of the Hebrew *kabod* is heavy in weight. The verb often comes to mean 'to give weight to, honor.'"[2]

Josh McClellan says, "The word kabod means weight or heaviness. Thus to experience the glory of God is to feel the weight of God. To know God's glory is for Him to be heavy upon us. It is a rich concept with a number of implications."[3]

We see weight and wealth connected in the book of Haggai:

> And I will shake all nations, and the desire of all nations shall come: and I will fill this house with glory, saith the LORD of hosts. The silver is mine, and the gold is mine, saith the LORD of hosts. The glory of this latter house shall be

133

greater than of the former, saith the LORD of hosts: and in this place will I give peace, saith the LORD of hosts.

—HAGGAI 2:7–9

Paul connects weight and glory in his epistle to the Corinthians:

For our light affliction, which is but for a moment, worketh for us a far more exceeding and eternal weight of glory;

—2 CORINTHIANS 4:17

Jesus spoke of the weightier matters of the law. *Weightier* means more important or heavier:

Woe unto you, scribes and Pharisees, hypocrites! for ye pay tithe of mint and anise and cummin, and have omitted the weightier matters of the law, judgment, mercy, and faith: these ought ye to have done, and not to leave the other undone.

—MATTHEW 23:23

God's glory is His weightiness, His heaviness, and His substance. The weight of glory is the weight of His presence. We can see some of our gatherings are weightier than others. The presence and glory are heavier at times. The glory can be so heavy until we cannot stand.

When the glory (*kabod*) comes upon you, think of it as the "heavyweight" anointing. It's the anointing to elevate you and upgrade you. But you will be face smashed on the floor when it happens.[4]

THE WEIGHT OF KINGS

In the Old Testament the prosperity of kings was determined by weight. Solomon was the wealthiest king of his day. Over six hundred talents of gold came to him yearly.

Now the weight of gold that came to Solomon in one year was six hundred threescore and six talents of gold.

—1 KINGS 10:14

A talent was an ancient unit of weight and value in Greece, Rome, and the Middle East. In the Old Testament a talent was a unit of measurement for weighing precious metals, usually gold and silver. In the New Testament a talent was a value of money or coin.[5] Some estimates of the weight of a talent range between seventy-five and ninety-five pounds.

> And Hiram sent to the king sixscore talents of gold.
>
> —1 Kings 9:14

> And they came to Ophir, and fetched from thence gold, four hundred and twenty talents, and brought it to King Solomon.
>
> —1 Kings 9:28

Sheba brought gold by weight to Solomon. The weight of what she gave determined its value. Sheba gave a considerable amount by weight.

> And she gave the king an hundred and twenty talents of gold, and of spices very great store, and precious stones: there came no more such abundance of spices as these which the queen of Sheba gave to king Solomon.
>
> —1 Kings 10:10

A king's crown

> David took the crown from their king's head, and it was placed on his own head. It weighed a talent of gold, and it was set with precious stones.
>
> —2 Samuel 12:30, niv

David had a gold crown set on his head that was measured by weight. We can also wear a weighty crown of glory.

A king's words

The words of kings also carry weight. Kings decree. The king's word is law in his kingdom.

> Where the word of a king is, there is power: and who may say
> unto him, What doest thou?
>
> —Ecclesiastes 8:4

Weight and the Tabernacle

Another place we see the connection between weight and glory is
in the construction of the tabernacle in the wilderness:

> Of a talent of pure gold shall he make it, with all these vessels.
>
> —Exodus 25:39

> Of a talent of pure gold made he it, and all the vessels thereof.
>
> —Exodus 37:24

> All the gold that was occupied for the work in all the work
> of the holy place, even the gold of the offering, was twenty
> and nine talents, and seven hundred and thirty shekels, after
> the shekel of the sanctuary. And the silver of them that were
> numbered of the congregation was an hundred talents, and
> a thousand seven hundred and threescore and fifteen shekels,
> after the shekel of the sanctuary.
>
> —Exodus 38:24–25

> And of the hundred talents of silver were cast the sockets
> of the sanctuary, and the sockets of the vail; an hundred
> sockets of the hundred talents, a talent for a socket.
>
> —Exodus 38:27

> And the brass of the offering was seventy talents, and two
> thousand and four hundred shekels.
>
> —Exodus 38:29

Weight and the Temple

From the parcel of ground to the articles in the temple, they were
also all connected to weight.

David bought the threshing floor of Ornan, which would eventually become the site of the temple, for six hundred shekels of
gold. The place of the temple was purchased by weight:

So David gave to Ornan for the place six hundred shekels of gold by weight.

—1 Chronicles 21:25

And David prepared iron in abundance for the nails for the doors of the gates, and for the joinings; and brass in abundance without weight.

—1 Chronicles 22:3

Now, behold, in my trouble I have prepared for the house of the Lord an hundred thousand talents of gold, and a thousand thousand talents of silver; and of brass and iron without weight; for it is in abundance: timber also and stone have I prepared; and thou mayest add thereto.

—1 Chronicles 22:14

All the articles of the tabernacle were measured by weight:

He gave of gold by weight for things of gold, for all instruments of all manner of service; silver also for all instruments of silver by weight, for all instruments of every kind of service.

—1 Chronicles 28:14

Even the weight for the candlesticks of gold, and for their lamps of gold, by weight for every candlestick, and for the lamps thereof: and for the candlesticks of silver by weight, both for the candlestick, and also for the lamps thereof, according to the use of every candlestick.

—1 Chronicles 28:15

Candlesticks represent light and illumination. The weight of glory brings light and illumination.

And by weight he gave gold for the tables of shewbread, for every table; and likewise silver for the tables of silver.

—1 Chronicles 28:16

> Also pure gold for the fleshhooks, and the bowls, and the cups:
> and for the golden basons he gave gold by weight for every
> bason; and likewise silver by weight for every bason of silver:
>
> —1 Chronicles 28:17

The altar of incense also had weight. The altar represents prayer, worship, and sacrifice and signifies our prayers and worship should be weighty.

> And for the altar of incense refined gold by weight; and gold
> for the pattern of the chariot of the cherubims, that spread out
> their wings, and covered the ark of the covenant of the Lord.
>
> —1 Chronicles 28:18

> And the weight of the nails was fifty shekels of gold. And he
> overlaid the upper chambers with gold.
>
> —2 Chronicles 3:9

> Thus Solomon made all these vessels in great abundance: for
> the weight of the brass could not be found out.
>
> —2 Chronicles 4:18

Every vessel and furnishing in the house of God had weight. We are all vessels in the house of the Lord, and our prayers, worship, and sacrifice should carry the weight of glory. We *need* the weight of glory to be a part of God's temple.

Weight and Restoration

Weight also appears during the days of Ezra. Ezra was a part of restoration. Ezra was alive during the rebuilding of the temple. Weigh, weighs, weighted, or weight is mentioned in Ezra six times. (See the verses after the next sentence.) Haggai (a prophet of restoration) prophesied about the glory and connected it to gold and silver (Hag. 2:8–9).

> …and weighed unto them the silver, and the gold, and the
> vessels, even the offering of the house of our God, which the
> king, and his counsellors, and his lords, and all Israel there

present, had offered: I even weighed unto their hand six hundred and fifty talents of silver, and silver vessels an hundred talents, and of gold an hundred talents.... Watch ye, and keep them, until ye weigh them before the chief of the priests and the Levites, and chief of the fathers of Israel, at Jerusalem, in the chambers of the house of the LORD. So took the priests and the Levites the weight of the silver, and the gold, and the vessels, to bring them to Jerusalem unto the house of our God.... Now on the fourth day was the silver and the gold and the vessels weighed in the house of our God by the hand of Meremoth the son of Uriah the priest; and with him was Eleazar the son of Phinehas; and with them was Jozabad the son of Jeshua, and Noadiah the son of Binnui, Levites; by number and by weight of every one: and all the weight was written at that time.

—EZRA 8:25–26, 29–30, 33–34

When restoration comes to your life, weight (wealth, power, and influence) returns. The glory makes you weighty. Zion is the place of weight because it is the place of glory.

THE WEIGHTY MAN

Psalm 112 describes the prosperous man. Wealth and riches are in his house. I call this man the weighty man.

His seed shall be mighty upon earth: the generation of the upright shall be blessed. Wealth and riches shall be in his house: and his righteousness endureth for ever.

—PSALM 112:2–3

A weighty man is not only a man of wealth but a man of influence. Job was a weighty man—wealthy and influential. Job describes his influence before he went into captivity. Job was the wealthiest and most powerful man of his generation:

Moreover Job continued his parable, and said, Oh that I were as in months past, as in the days when God preserved me;

when his candle shined upon my head, and when by his light
I walked through darkness; as I was in the days of my youth,
when the secret of God was upon my tabernacle; when the
Almighty was yet with me, when my children were about me;
when I washed my steps with butter, and the rock poured me
out rivers of oil; when I went out to the gate through the city,
when I prepared my seat in the street! The young men saw
me, and hid themselves: and the aged arose, and stood up.
The princes refrained talking, and laid their hand on their
mouth. The nobles held their peace, and their tongue cleaved
to the roof of their mouth. When the ear heard me, then it
blessed me; and when the eye saw me, it gave witness to me.

—Job 29:1–11

God's candle (light and glory) shined upon Job's head. Job was
prosperous, influential, and respected. Job's words carried weight.
People stopped talking when Job showed up, and when they heard
his words, they were blessed. Job's word carried weight.

Job described the days when his glory and honor were fresh and
being constantly renewed:

My glory and honor are fresh in me [being constantly
renewed], And my bow gains [ever] new strength in my hand.

—Job 29:20, amp

Job felt he lost his weightiness (glory) when he was under attack
by Satan:

He hath stripped me of my glory, and taken the crown from
my head.

—Job 19:9

Job's weight was restored when God "turned [his] captivity" (Job
42:10).

Apostolic and Prophetic Weight

There is a weight in the apostolic ministry. Apostles' words and messages are weighty. The gifts and anointing have weight, so they have spiritual influence and power:

> For his letters, say they, are weighty and powerful; but his bodily presence is weak, and his speech contemptible.
> —2 Corinthians 10:10

The words of Jesus certainly carried weight, and his anointing has weight (Isa. 61:1).

> And they were astonished at his doctrine: for his word was with power.
> —Luke 4:32

> And they were all amazed, and spake among themselves, saying, What a word is this! for with authority and power he commandeth the unclean spirits, and they come out.
> —Luke 4:36

> The centurion answered and said, Lord, I am not worthy that thou shouldest come under my roof: but speak the word only, and my servant shall be healed.
> —Matthew 8:8

The apostle's word carries weight. Your words can be weighty. These words carry force and impact. The glory will affect our words.

> And my speech and my preaching was not with enticing words of man's wisdom, but in demonstration of the Spirit and of power.
> —1 Corinthians 2:4

> While Peter yet spake these words, the Holy Ghost fell on all them which heard the word.
> —Acts 10:44

The prophet's word carries weight. Prophecy carries weight. The prophetic word has power.

> And the elders of the Jews builded, and they prospered through the prophesying of Haggai the prophet and Zechariah the son of Iddo.
>
> —Ezra 6:14

> But truly I am full of power by the spirit of the Lord, and of judgment, and of might, to declare unto Jacob his transgression, and to Israel his sin.
>
> —Micah 3:8

> Is not my word like as a fire? saith the Lord; and like a hammer that breaketh the rock in pieces?
>
> —Jeremiah 23:29

Apostolic men and women of this age have weight. What is the weight of your ministry? What is the weight of your message? The Urban Dictionary defines a *heavyweight* as:

> Someone who is highly respected or famous owing to their deep knowledge of an academic subject or influence in society. When a heavyweight writes, speaks or comments on their specialized subject, people listen, record, share and Tweet their views.[6]

Even as the words of apostles and prophets carry weight, all the members of our churches should have weight. Zion churches have weight, and that weight influences people for the kingdom.

WEIGHT OF GLORY CONFESSIONS

Lord, let the weight of Your glory rest upon my life.

Let Your weighty presence be upon my life.

Let the weight of Your glory be upon my tabernacle.

Let Your weight bring wealth into my life.

Let my words carry weight.

Let my decrees have weight.

Let our churches carry the weight of Your glory.

Let our praise and worship be weighty.

Let our prayers be weighty.

Let our prophetic utterances be weighty.

Let our messages be weighty.

Let Your weight bring influence to my life.

Let me be able to handle weighty issues.

Let the weight of Your glory bring great blessings.

Let the weight of Your glory release deliverance.

Let the weight of Your glory release healing.

Let the weight of Your glory bring revival.

Chapter 10

THE AUTHORITY AND STRENGTH OF THE ZION BELIEVER

*Then you will see and be radiant, and your heart will tremble
[with joy] and rejoice Because the abundant wealth of the seas will
be brought to you, the wealth of the nations will come to you.*
—ISAIAH 60:5, AMP

THE HEBREW WORD *chayil* is the secret behind the strength,
wealth, spiritual military might, and virtue of the Zion believer.
Zion believers know how to create and rule their world. *Rule* is the
Hebrew word for *dominion*, which means to tread down, to subdue;
to crumble; to create; to make; to prevail against, to reign, to rule
and to take.[1] In other words, you, as the Zion believer, should use
your authority to defend, acquire, manage, and steward what is
yours (yourself, family, possessions, wealth, and destiny) and protect
your personal prosperity and dignity. In this chapter I will show how
chayil performs in your life as you put on the Zion identity.

CHAYIL

Chayil is an amazing Hebrew word that represents many aspects of
power and might, including wealth. I began to preach on this word
chayil while ministering from Proverbs chapter 31 on the virtuous
woman. The word *virtuous* is the way the King James Version
translates the Hebrew word *chayil*. It is one of only three times the
word is translated "virtuous" in the King James Version:

> *Eshet Chayil* means "woman of worth," "valor," or "strength."
> The phrase comes from Proverbs 31:10, where it introduces

a paean to her manifold virtues. "Who can find her," the author asks rhetorically. She rises while it's still night to bring food for her household, her lamp never goes out, her mouth is full of wisdom, and teachings of lovingkindness are on her tongue, and much, much more.[2]

—Rabbi Julian Sinclair

Ish-chayil means a mighty man, a valiant man.[3] The word for *valiant warrior* or *mighty warrior* is *gibbor chayil* in the Hebrew. According to Tim Brown, founder of REUP men's ministry, "It's the same word used to describe David's mighty group of fighting men."[4]

Chayil is also translated "army" fifty-six times.[5] The word *army* represents military strength, might, and power. The word is translated as "forces" in Isaiah 60, which means wealth and riches. The word *forces* also brings to mind the term *armed forces*, which connects it to the word *army*. There are many other meanings as well:

> *Chayil* is a Hebrew word that is rich, powerful, and glorious. Its many meanings are found in 243 references in the Bible such as strength, active, activated, courage, power, force, dominion, elite army, wealth, efficiency, praiseworthy, excellence, wisdom, virtue, moral worth, honor, ability, capable, special forces, great, mighty, troops, host, valiant, valor, warriors, company, trained, noble, preference, favor, full, goods, retinue, riches, substance, territory, influence. According to *Strong's Concordance*, its three key meanings are power, wealth, and army and its strongest meaning is army.[6]
>
> —Pat Francis

CHAYIL AND ZION

Because Zion is chayil and you are Zion, you are chayil. The Scriptures reveal the richness of the word, and how it is connected to the glory and Zion.

The first time the word *chayil* is in Scripture is Genesis 34:29. Here the word is translated as "wealth." The word is translated as "wealth" ten times, "riches" eleven times, and "substance" eight times in the King James Version.[7]

Another important translation of the word *chayil* is "valor." A chayil man is a man of valor. A chayil woman is a woman of valor. The word, therefore, represents strength, might, power, and courage.

Individuals can possess chayil. Nations and cities can possess chayil. Leaders and kings possess chayil. David, the king, had chayil. Chayil comes from God.

> Both riches and honour come of thee, and thou reignest over all; and in thine hand is power and might; and in thine hand it is to make great, and to give strength unto all.
>
> —1 Chronicles 29:12

God gave Solomon riches and wisdom. Solomon's fame was known throughout the world. Chayil came to him from the queen of Sheba. Solomon is a type of Christ and the kingdom. Solomon is a picture of chayil coming to Zion.

> But thou shalt remember the Lord thy God: for it is he that giveth thee power to get wealth, that he may establish his covenant which he sware unto thy fathers, as it is this day.
>
> —Deuteronomy 8:18

Wealth in this verse is the word *chayil*. Chayil is financial power and strength. This is what comes to Zion—the wealth of the nations. Zion is a wealthy place. You are Zion. God gives you the power to get wealth.

+ Chayil is valor. Valor is courage and boldness. Gideon was called a mighty man of valor (chayil). You are Zion. You are a person of valor.

+ Chayil is an army, a force. Zion is an elite army. The Lord is the Lord of armies. Zion is a fortress with an army of mighty warriors. Zion is an army with banners (Song of Sol. 6:4, 10). You are Zion. You are elite.

- Chayil is ability. Able men were chayil men. Zion believers have ability. You are Zion. You are able.

- Chayil is influence. Zion has influence. Zion is an influential city. Zion believers are influencers. You are Zion. You are an influencer.

- Chayil is wisdom. Chayil is honor. Wisdom is connected to promotion, wealth, riches, and honor. You are Zion. You have wisdom. You have honor.

- Chayil is efficiency, "a system of maximum productivity with minimum wasted effort or expense;" "businesslike," "competent," "productive," "capable," "organized."[8] Chayil believers are efficient.

FROM STRENGTH TO STRENGTH

They go from strength to strength, every one of them in Zion appeareth before God.

—Psalm 84:7

Strength in this verse is translated from chayil. We go from chayil to chayil. There are different levels of chayil. The Amplified Bible translates this verse like this: "They go from strength to strength [increasing in victorious power]." The Wycliffe translation says, "…from virtue into virtue." Chayil is virtue. Virtue is power and strength. Jesus felt virtue leave His body when the woman touched the hem of His garment (Luke 8:46).

God has called us the glory and virtue (2 Pet. 1:3). Glory and virtue are connected in Scripture. The multitudes were healed because virtue was released (Luke 6:19). Zion is the place of virtue. You are Zion. You are virtuous.

Chayil also means valiant.

Through God we shall do valiantly: for he it is that shall tread down our enemies

—Psalm 108:13

Zion believers are valiant. We do valiantly through God. We tread down the enemy through chayil.

Chayil means wealth.

> A good man leaveth an inheritance to his children's children:
> and the wealth of the sinner is laid up for the just.
> —PROVERBS 13:22

The wealth (chayil) comes to Zion. You are Zion. Chayil comes to you.

Chayil is also translated "might" six times in the King James Version.[9] Zion is the place of power and might. People bring their might (chayil) to Zion. You are Zion. You have the spirit of might. The God of Zion is the mighty God.

THE SPIRIT OF MIGHT

I was preaching recently about the strength of the ox. As I concluded the message, I invited people who felt the need for more strength to come to the front for prayer and ministry. As I prayed, I received a word of knowledge concerning might. I then prayed for might to come upon believers to have strength and power to accomplish God's will for their lives.

A fellow minister told me afterward that his message for the next day was on apostolic might. He was amazed at the word of knowledge concerning might and also said there were few messages being preached on this subject.

I then began to do a study on might and was amazed at the many scriptural references to this subject. Isaiah's prophecy concerning Jesus the Messiah also mentions the spirit of might:

> And the spirit of the LORD shall rest upon him, the spirit of wisdom and understanding, the spirit of counsel and might, the spirit of knowledge and of the fear of the LORD.
> —ISAIAH 11:2

Might is often translated from the Hebrew word *gĕbuwrah*, meaning "force (literally or figuratively); by implication, valor, victory:—force, mastery, might, mighty (act, power), power, strength. The KJV translates this word in the following manner: might (27x), strength (17x), power (9x), mighty acts (4x), mighty (2x), force (1x), mastery (1x)."[10]

The Greek word for *might* or *power* is *dunamis*. *Dunamis* means "strength, power, ability, inherent power, power residing in a thing by virtue of its nature, or which a person or thing exerts and puts forth power for performing miracles, moral power, and excellence of soul; the power and influence which belong to riches and wealth, power and resources arising from numbers, power consisting in or resting upon armies, forces, hosts."[11] *Dunamis* is used 120 times in the KJV and is translated "power" (77x), "mighty work" (11x), "strength" (7x), "miracle" (7x), "might" (4x), "virtue" (3x), "mighty" (2x), or miscellaneous (9x).[12] We will examine other words that will give you a greater understanding of might.

The Holy Spirit is a Spirit of might. Those who have received the Holy Spirit can operate in the spirit of might.

Over the next several pages I will explain the different manifestations of might and how it manifests in the life of a Zion believer, and I will stir your faith to believe for might to operate in your life.

Biblical might is connected to wisdom, counsel, glory, victory, breakthrough, wind, prophecy, miracles, healing, deliverance, preaching, and teaching.

The spirit of might is not human strength or might but the might that comes from the Holy Spirit.

> Then he answered and spake unto me, saying, This is the word of the LORD unto Zerubbabel, saying, Not by might, nor by power, but by my spirit, saith the LORD of hosts.
> —ZECHARIAH 4:6

Zechariah prophesied to Zerubbabel that what he had to accomplish would be by the Spirit and not by human might. What seemed impossible would be possible. God uses insignificant people to display his might and power.

Might is God's strength or power. God is known for strength and is called the mighty God (El Gibbor), as is Jesus (Isa. 9:6).

The psalmist asks, "Who is the King of glory? The LORD strong and *mighty* [gibborw], the LORD mighty in battle. Lift up your heads, O gates, and lift them up, O ancient doors, that the King of glory may come in! Who is this King of glory? The LORD of hosts, He is the King of glory. Selah" (Ps. 24:8–10, NASB, emphasis added).

> Gird Your sword on Your thigh, O Mighty [gibborw] One, in Your splendor and Your majesty!
> —PSALM 45:3, NASB

> Behold, God is mighty, and despiseth not any: he is mighty in strength and wisdom.
> —JOB 36:5

In Genesis God is referred to as the Mighty One of Jacob.

> But his bow remained firm, and his arms were agile, from the hands of the Mighty One of Jacob (From there is the Shepherd, the Stone of Israel).
> —GENESIS 49:24, NASB

> …how he swore to the LORD, and vowed to the Mighty One of Jacob.
> —PSALM 132:2, NASB

> …until I find a place for the LORD, a dwelling place for the Mighty One of Jacob.
> —PSALM 132:5, GW

His gods (magistrates and rulers) are also mighty:

> God standeth in the congregation of the mighty; he judgeth among the gods.
> —PSALM 82:1

> God stands in the assembly [of the representatives] of God;
> in the midst of the magistrates or judges He gives judgment
> [as] among the gods.
>
> —Psalm 82:1, ampc

Some believe these gods (*elohim*[13]) are divine beings (fallen angels). Angels also excel in strength (might).

> Bless the Lord, ye his angels, that excel in strength, that do
> his commandments, hearkening unto the voice of his word.
>
> —Psalm 103:20

The word *excel* is the Hebrew word *gibborw*, which means "powerful; by implication, warrior, tyrant:—champion, chief, excel, giant, man, mighty (man, one), strong (man), valiant man."[14] Kurt Selles explains:

> The Hebrew word *gibbor*, meaning "strong, mighty," describes
> heroes like Nimrod, "a mighty warrior…a mighty hunter
> before the Lord" (Genesis 10:8–9), and the "mighty warriors"
> of King David of Israel (2 Samuel 23:8). It's a word depicting
> bravery, courage, and action. All these are qualities of gibbor
> in the compound name El Gibbor, "the Mighty God."[15]

Might originates with God and is transferred to the angelic realm and the human realm.

Kings and Might

David, the son of Jesse, was known as a mighty, valiant man. The Lord was with him. Might, in this case, has to do with war and fighting.

> Then answered one of the servants, and said, Behold, I have
> seen a son of Jesse the Bethlehemite, that is cunning in
> playing, and a mighty valiant man, and a man of war, and
> prudent in matters, and a comely person, and the Lord is
> with him.
>
> —1 Samuel 16:18

We learn more about David's might in Psalm 18:

> He teacheth my hands to war, so that a bow of steel is broken by mine arms.
>
> —Psalm 18:34

> For thou hast girded me with strength unto the battle: thou hast subdued under me those that rose up against me.
>
> —Psalm 18:39

When David was anointed by Samuel, the spirit of might came upon him. David describes himself as being girded, or clothed, with strength. *Strength* here is the Hebrew word *chayil*, meaning probably "a force, whether of men, means or other resources; an army, wealth, virtue, valor, strength:—able, activity, army, band of men (soldiers), company, (great) forces, goods, host, might, power, riches, strength, strong, substance, train, valiant(-ly), valour, virtuous(-ly), war, worthy(-ily)."[16] *Chayil* is translated as "forces" in Isaiah 60:5, 11. This word applies to military might as seen in the term *armed forces*.

Might is force. Force is strength or energy as an attribute of physical action or movement.[17] Synonyms for *force* include *strength, power, energy, might, potency, vigor, muscle, stamina, effort, exertion, impact, pressure, weight, impetus,* and *punch*.[18] Force is connected to strength and might.

Kings were known for their might. Kings were known for their armies and their ability to fight. David was known for his might, as were his mighty men.

> These be the names of the mighty men whom David had: The Tachmonite that sat in the seat, chief among the captains; the same was Adino the Eznite: he lift up his spear against eight hundred, whom he slew at one time. And after him was Eleazar the son of Dodo the Ahohite, one of the three mighty men with David, when they defied the Philistines

that were there gathered together to battle, and the men of Israel were gone away.

—2 Samuel 23:8–9

And the three mighty men brake through the host of the Philistines, and drew water out of the well of Bethlehem, that was by the gate, and took it, and brought it to David: nevertheless he would not drink thereof, but poured it out unto the Lord.

—2 Samuel 23:16

These mighty men did great exploits. The spirit of might upon David was also upon these mighty men. I believe the spirit of might can be imparted. Might will give you great victories. Might will give you the ability to defeat the enemy and help you overcome overwhelming odds:

For by thee I have run through a troop; and by my God have I leaped over a wall.

—Psalm 18:29

David describes his might in Psalm 18, and he attributes his might to God:

I have pursued mine enemies, and overtaken them: neither did I turn again till they were consumed. I have wounded them that they were not able to rise: they are fallen under my feet. For thou hast girded me with strength unto the battle: thou hast subdued under me those that rose up against me. Thou hast also given me the necks of mine enemies; that I might destroy them that hate me. They cried, but there was none to save them: even unto the Lord, but he answered them not. Then did I beat them small as the dust before the wind: I did cast them out as the dirt in the streets.

—Psalm 18:37–42

David repeatedly refers to God as his strength. David was a chayil man.

> The Lord is my rock, and my fortress, and my deliverer; my God, my strength, in whom I will trust; my buckler, and the horn of my salvation, and my high tower.
>
> —Psalm 18:2

> The Lord is my light and my salvation; whom shall I fear? the Lord is the strength of my life; of whom shall I be afraid?
>
> —Psalm 27:1

The spirit of might is the strength of the Lord. It is not human strength, but the strength given by the Spirit of God. This strength was his fortress and protection. This might was the key to David's victories.

Jehoshaphat was also known for his might. Jehoshaphat was a chayil man.

> Now the rest of the acts of Jehoshaphat, and his might that he shewed, and how he warred, are they not written in the book of the chronicles of the kings of Judah?
>
> —1 Kings 22:45

Jehu was known for his might. Jehu was the king who challenged Jezebel and had her thrown from the window. It took might to defeat and destroy Jezebel.

> Now the rest of the acts of Jehu, and all that he did, and all his might, are they not written in the book of the chronicles of the kings of Israel?
>
> —2 Kings 10:34

Hezekiah was known for his might. Hezekiah was a chayil man.

> And the rest of the acts of Hezekiah, and all his might, and how he made a pool, and a conduit, and brought water into the city, are they not written in the book of the chronicles of the kings of Judah?
>
> —2 Kings 20:20

God has also made us kings and priests in Zion, and because the spirit of might operates in kings, the spirit of might will give you dominion. The spirit of might will make you a champion.

THE HOLY SPIRIT AND MIGHT

When Jesus came out of the wilderness after forty days of fasting, He cast out devils through the power of the Holy Spirit.

> And Jesus returned in the power of the Spirit into Galilee: and there went out a fame of him through all the region round about.
>
> —LUKE 4:14

Jesus cast out devils by the Spirit of God. He bound the strongman. Might made Him stronger than the strongman.

> But if I cast out devils by the Spirit of God, then the kingdom of God is come unto you. Or else how can one enter into a strong man's house, and spoil his goods, except he first bind the strong man? Then he will spoil his house.
>
> —MATTHEW 12:28–29

Jesus cast devils out of many (Mark 1:34; Luke 4:41). Deliverance occurs because of might.

Jesus walked in the power of the Holy Spirit throughout His ministry. Jesus was mighty in word and deed.

> And he said unto them, What things? And they said unto him, Concerning Jesus of Nazareth, which was a prophet mighty in deed and word before God and all the people.
>
> —LUKE 24:19

The spirit of might can manifest in your speech and your actions. Jesus spoke with power, healed with power, and delivered the bound with power. Power (might) is released through words and action.

Jesus was a prophet like Moses, and Moses was also mighty in word and deed:

> And Moses was learned in all the wisdom of the Egyptians,
> and was mighty in words and in deeds.
>
> —ACTS 7:22

Moses operated in the spirit of might to deliver people from Pharaoh, and Jesus operated in the spirit of might to deliver people from Satan. The spirit of might manifested in the casting out of demons. Jesus gave His disciples the power (dunamis) to cast out demons and heal the sick (Luke 9:1).

Jesus displayed might in the cities of Israel. Jesus pronounced judgment upon the cities that did not repent after seeing these mighty works.

> Then began he to upbraid the cities wherein most of his
> mighty works were done, because they repented not: Woe
> unto thee, Chorazin! woe unto thee, Bethsaida! for if the
> mighty works, which were done in you, had been done in
> Tyre and Sidon, they would have repented long ago in sack-
> cloth and ashes.
>
> —MATTHEW 11:20–21

> And thou, Capernaum, which art exalted unto heaven, shalt
> be brought down to hell: for if the mighty works, which have
> been done in thee, had been done in Sodom, it would have
> remained until this day.
>
> —MATTHEW 11:23

The phrase *mighty works* in both scriptures is from the Greek word *dunamis* (or *dynamis* in some lexicons), meaning "force (literally or figuratively); specially, miraculous power (usually by implication, a miracle itself):—ability, abundance, meaning, might (-ily, deed), (worker of) miracle (-s), power, strength, violence, mighty (wonderful) work."[19]

> And as he was yet a coming, the devil threw him down, and
> tare him. And Jesus rebuked the unclean spirit, and healed
> the child, and delivered him again to his father. And they
> were all amazed at the mighty power of God. But while they

wondered every one at all things which Jesus did, he said unto his disciples…

—LUKE 9:42–43

The phrase *mighty power* is another Greek word, *megaleiotēs*, which means "greatness, magnificence of the majesty of God, of the visible splendour of the divine majesty as it appeared in the transfiguration of Christ."[20] In other words, might (or power) is connected to glory. *Mega* is a part of this word. *Mega* means great. *Mega* also means mighty. Might is mega power. I will discuss the relationship between *mega*, *might*, and *glory* again later.

There is an anointing for might. Jesus was anointed with the Holy Ghost and power:

> God anointed Jesus of Nazareth with the Holy Ghost and with power: who went about doing good, and healing all that were oppressed of the devil; for God was with him.
>
> —ACTS 10:38

Because of the anointing, Jesus went about doing good and healing all who were oppressed of the devil. Might is connected to both healing and deliverance. David was also anointed:

> Then Samuel took the horn of oil, and anointed him in the midst of his brethren: and the Spirit of the LORD came upon David from that day forward. So Samuel rose up, and went to Ramah.
>
> —1 SAMUEL 16:13

To *anoint* means "to smear or rub with oil."[21] Oil is a symbol of the Holy Spirit. The oil of God gives us might and power.

FAITH AND MIGHT

I cannot overemphasize the importance of faith when dealing with the spirit of might.

> And he could there do no mighty work, save that he laid his
> hands upon a few sick folk, and healed them.
> —Mark 6:5

This verse reveals the spirit of might cannot function in an atmosphere of unbelief. Jesus did a few minor miracles, but He could do no mighty works in His hometown. Faith is the atmosphere where the spirit of might can manifest. Faith will cause the spirit of might to operate in your life.

Preaching the Word produces faith, which in turn makes way for the spirit of might. Jesus preached the good news and operated in the spirit of might. The gospel opens the way for the spirit of might to operate, resulting in mighty works.

> And Stephen, full of faith and power, did great wonders and
> miracles among the people.
> —Acts 6:8

Stephen did great wonders and miracles because he was filled with faith and power. This shows the relationship between faith and might.

> And what the exceeding greatness of his power to us-ward
> who believe, according to that working of the strength of his
> might.
> —Ephesians 1:19, asv

God's power and might are available to those who believe. Paul prayed for a revelation of this might and power to those who believe. Do you believe? Do you have faith for might to operate in your life? Do you have a revelation of might? Hopefully this book will stir your faith and open your eyes to the spirit of might.

Wait for Power

The disciples were told to wait in Jerusalem and go nowhere until they received power and might.

And, behold, I send the promise of my Father upon you: but tarry ye in the city of Jerusalem, until ye be endued with power from on high.

—Luke 24:49

Power is promised to us. This promise was fulfilled on the day of Pentecost.

But ye shall receive power, after that the Holy Ghost is come upon you: and ye shall be witnesses unto me both in Jerusalem, and in all Judaea, and in Samaria, and unto the uttermost part of the earth.

—Acts 1:8

The day of Pentecost and the outpouring of the Holy Spirit was the release of the spirit of might. There was the sound of a rushing mighty wind. The wind is a symbol of power and might.

And suddenly there came a sound from heaven as of a rushing mighty wind, and it filled all the house where they were sitting.

—Acts 2:2

The believers received power (dunamis). The outpouring of the Holy Spirit was the outpouring of the spirit of might. The Book of Acts chronicles the might of the church. Might is not only for individuals but also for churches.

Even the youths shall faint and be weary, and the young men shall utterly fall: But they that wait upon the LORD shall renew their strength; they shall mount up with wings as eagles; they shall run, and not be weary; and they shall walk, and not faint.

—Isaiah 40:30–31

Wait upon the Lord and renew your strength (might). Strength and might are the antidote for weariness and tiredness. *Wait* is from the Hebrew word *qavah*, meaning "to bind together (perhaps by twisting), i.e., collect; (figuratively) to expect:—gather (together), look, patiently, tarry, wait (for, on, upon)."[22]

We can receive the spirit of might through gathering and waiting for and expecting the Lord's power. To *wait* also means "to linger."[23] There are times we need to linger in the presence of the Lord. We wait in faith with the expectation of the Lord's might and power. Wait also means to be "strong, robust (from the notion of binding fast)."[24]

APOSTOLIC MIGHT

> …and with great power gave the apostles witness of the resurrection of the Lord Jesus: and great grace was upon them all.
>
> —ACTS 4:33

The apostles operated in great power. This is mega power. Notice in this verse that power is connected to grace. The apostles had mega power and mega grace.

> …through mighty signs and wonders, by the power of the Spirit of God; so that from Jerusalem, and round about unto Illyricum, I have fully preached the gospel of Christ.
>
> —ROMANS 15:19

> …(For the weapons of our warfare are not carnal, but mighty through God to the pulling down of strong holds;) Casting down imaginations, and every high thing that exalteth itself against the knowledge of God, and bringing into captivity every thought to the obedience of Christ;
>
> —2 CORINTHIANS 10:4–5

Warfare is the Greek word *strateia* meaning "military service, i.e. (figuratively) the apostolic career (as one of hardship and danger):—warfare."[25] Paul identifies the apostolic career as mighty to pull down strongholds. *Strongholds* is the Greek word *ochuróma* meaning "a fortress, strong defense, stronghold."[26]

Paul then identifies the strongholds as imaginations. *Imaginations* is the Greek word *logismos,* meaning "a thought, reasoning or an argument."[27] These are arguments in the minds of people who are resistant to truth. They are the "'bottom-line' reasoning that reflects someone's values, i.e., how they personally assign weight in determining what they find reasonable;" "a reasoning: such as is hostile to the Christian faith."[28] These arguments (philosophies, mindsets) are reinforced by demons. They prevent people from obeying the truth. The apostle has to have the might to challenge these arguments and cast them down. It takes might to accomplish this. It takes mighty preaching and teaching to confront these arguments. We will discuss being mighty in Scripture later.

The apostolic ministry is not limited to preaching, but also demonstrating the might of God.

> Truly the signs of an apostle were wrought among you in all patience, in signs, and wonders, and mighty deeds.
> —2 Corinthians 12:12

Paul calls these mighty deeds. The phrase *mighty deeds* is from the Greek word *dunamis.* The spirit of might manifests in miracles. This might validates true apostles.

You cannot separate apostolic ministry from might and power. Paul also mentions patience. Patience is perseverance and endurance. It takes might and strength to endure. Remember Paul likened the apostolic ministry to military service.

The spirit of might operates through apostolic preaching. There is a demonstration of the Spirit and power through apostolic ministry.

> And my speech and my preaching was not with enticing words of man's wisdom, but in demonstration of the Spirit and of power.
> —1 Corinthians 2:4

> By the word of truth, by the power of God, by the armour of righteousness on the right hand and on the left.
> —2 Corinthians 6:7

PROPHETIC MIGHT

Prophets also operate in might. They declare the Word of the Lord with might. Prophets have chayil.

> But truly I am full of power by the spirit of the LORD, and of judgment, and of might, to declare unto Jacob his transgression, and to Israel his sin.
>
> —MICAH 3:8

Prophetic utterances carry power and might. God's Word in the mouth of a prophet is like a hammer that breaks the rock in pieces. Elijah was a prophet who walked in power, and John the Baptizer came in the spirit and power of Elijah:

> And he shall go before him in the spirit and power of Elias, to turn the hearts of the fathers to the children, and the disobedient to the wisdom of the just; to make ready a people prepared for the Lord.
>
> —LUKE 1:17

The spirit of might working through John brought the people to repentance. He preached with power and turned hearts. Mighty preaching will turn the hearts of people.

People were astonished at Jesus' powerful teaching.

> And they were astonished at his doctrine: for his word was with power.
>
> —LUKE 4:32

> They were surprised at his teaching because he taught them as if he had the right to teach them.
>
> —LUKE 4:32, WE

The word translated "power" is the Greek word *exousia*, which means "authority."[29] Might operates with authority. Authority is the legal right to use power and might.[30]

Prophets have the right to speak on behalf of God. Their words carry power. I call this prophetic might. The prophetic word has the power to change things and to shift and realign. One word of power can change your life. The prophetic word can bring healing and deliverance. A prophetic word can release you into your destiny. Remember, Jesus was mighty in word and deed.

Might and the Word of God

The spirit of might is also connected to the Word of God.

> For the word of God is quick, and powerful, and sharper than any twoedged sword, piercing even to the dividing asunder of soul and spirit, and of the joints and marrow, and is a discerner of the thoughts and intents of the heart.
>
> —Hebrews 4:12

Might is released through the preaching and teaching of the Word of God. Notice how healing is connected to preaching in the following verses.

> And Jesus went about all Galilee, teaching in their synagogues, and preaching the gospel of the kingdom, and healing all manner of sickness and all manner of disease among the people.
>
> —Matthew 4:23

> And Jesus went about all the cities and villages, teaching in their synagogues, and preaching the gospel of the kingdom, and healing every sickness and every disease among the people.
>
> —Matthew 9:35

> And they departed, and went through the towns, preaching the gospel, and healing every where.
>
> —Luke 9:6

Mary called Magdalene was healed of seven devils as a result of the preaching of the gospel.

> And it came to pass afterward, that he went throughout every city and village, preaching and shewing the glad tidings of the kingdom of God: and the twelve were with him,

> And certain women, which had been healed of evil spirits and infirmities, Mary called Magdalene, out of whom went seven devils.
>
> —Luke 8:1–2

Those who heard Jesus were healed and delivered from unclean spirits. The spirit of might will drive out sickness and disease.

> And he came down with them, and stood in the plain, and the company of his disciples, and a great multitude of people out of all Judaea and Jerusalem, and from the sea coast of Tyre and Sidon, which came to hear him, and to be healed of their diseases; and they that were vexed with unclean spirits: and they were healed. And the whole multitude sought to touch him: for there went virtue out of him, and healed them all.
>
> —Luke 6:17–19

Apollos was mighty in the Scriptures. Other translations say he was powerful, educated, and eloquent in the Scriptures.

> And a certain Jew named Apollos, born at Alexandria, an eloquent man, and mighty in the scriptures, came to Ephesus.
>
> —Acts 18:24

We can be mighty in the Word. We can and should be strong in the Word of God. We should be strong in revelation and understanding.

WISDOM AND MIGHT

Chayil is wisdom and might. Wisdom and might are linked together in Scripture.

> Counsel is mine, and sound wisdom: I am understanding; I have strength.
>
> —Proverbs 8:14

Wisdom has strength. *Strength* is the Hebrew word *geburah*, meaning "might."[31] The spirit of might is coupled with the spirit of wisdom. Wisdom is coupled with mighty acts in the ministry of Christ. Wisdom gives you might and strength.

> And when he was come into his own country, he taught them in their synagogue, insomuch that they were astonished, and said, Whence hath this man this wisdom, and these mighty works?
>
> —MATTHEW 13:54

The spirit of might is coupled with the spirit of counsel in Isaiah 11:2. *Counsel* is the Hebrew word *etsah*, meaning "advice; by implication, plan; also prudence:—advice, advisement, counsel(-lor), purpose."[32]

> A wise man is strong; yea, a man of knowledge increaseth strength.
>
> —PROVERBS 24:5

> Wisdom strengtheneth the wise more than ten mighty men which are in the city.
>
> —ECCLESIASTES 7:19

I believe wisdom is necessary to handle might. People with no wisdom would abuse and misuse might. God gives both wisdom and might.

Daniel also experienced wisdom and might.

> Daniel answered and said, Blessed be the name of God for ever and ever: for wisdom and might are his.
>
> —DANIEL 2:20

> I thank thee, and praise thee, O thou God of my fathers, who hast given me wisdom and might, and hast made known unto me now what we desired of thee: for thou hast now made known unto us the king's matter.
>
> —DANIEL 2:23

PRAYER AND MIGHT

Prayer has always been a source of great might and power. The early church prayed until the building shook. Prayer releases the might of God.

> And when they had prayed, the place was shaken where they were assembled together; and they were all filled with the Holy Ghost, and they spake the word of God with boldness.
>
> —ACTS 4:31

The result of this prayer was the apostles ministered in great power (mega power—Acts 4:33). The apostles gave themselves continually to prayer and the ministry of the word. Prayer and the Word will release the spirit of might (Acts 6:4).

Elijah also prayed with power and might. He prayed for the heavens to be closed, and he prayed for the heavens to be opened.

> Elias was a man subject to like passions as we are, and he prayed earnestly that it might not rain: and it rained not on the earth by the space of three years and six months. And he prayed again, and the heaven gave rain, and the earth brought forth her fruit.
>
> —JAMES 5:17–18

I believe the spirit of might makes us mighty in prayer. Mighty prayer is a key to breakthrough and miracles. Mighty prayer is strong prayer. The spirit of might will strengthen your prayer life. Strong believers make strong intercessors.

ZION IS THE PLACE OF ANSWERED PRAYER

We see God's favor on Zion to make our prayers mighty so they will be accepted. Prayers are answered in Zion. Isaiah 65:24 says, "And it shall come to pass, that before they call, I will answer; and while they are yet speaking, I will hear."

You are Zion. God hears your prayers. He answers while you are speaking—what a tremendous promise.

The LORD hear thee in the day of trouble; the name of the
God of Jacob defend thee; send thee help from the sanctuary,
and strengthen thee out of Zion; remember all thy offerings,
and accept thy burnt sacrifice; Selah. Grant thee according
to thine own heart, and fulfil all thy counsel.

—PSALM 20:1–4

God hears you in the day of trouble and strengthens you out of
Zion. God grants you according to your heart. He gives you what
you desire and fulfills all your plans.

Zion is the place of answered prayer. Zion is where we petition
God. Prayer is accepted in Zion.

O thou that hearest prayer, unto thee shall all flesh come.

—PSALM 65:2

People come to Zion because it is the place of answered prayer.
God hears prayer. The Contemporary English Version of the verse
above says, "Everyone will come to you because you answer prayer."
Zion is the place of God's presence and the place where He hears
and answers prayer.

Here is another powerful promise spoken through Isaiah.

Thus saith the LORD, In an acceptable time have I heard
thee, and in a day of salvation have I helped thee: and I will
preserve thee, and give thee for a covenant of the people, to
establish the earth, to cause to inherit the desolate heritages.

—ISAIAH 49:8

God's favor is in Zion because the "acceptable time" is the time
of favor. God hears you, He helps, and He saves you.

All the flocks of Kedar shall be gathered together unto thee,
the rams of Nebaioth shall minister unto thee: they shall
come up with acceptance on mine altar, and I will glorify the
house of my glory.

—ISAIAH 60:7

Notice the words "acceptance on mine altar." The altar represents prayer and worship. The Contemporary English Bible says, "They will be accepted on my altar." Zion is an accepted place. God accepts the outcasts, and God accepts their prayers.

This verse says the flocks of Kedar come. Kedar was the son of Ishmael (Gen. 25:13). The descendants of Ishmael come to Zion. Nations that once had no covenant relationship are drawn by Zion's glory.

The prayer of the upright is God's delight (Prov. 15:8). God's ears are open to the prayers of the righteous (1 Pet. 3:12). "The Lord is far from the wicked, but He hears the prayer of the righteous" (Prov. 15:29, NKJV).

Daniel prayed toward Jerusalem (Dan. 6:10). He did not forget Zion even though he was in Babylon. His heart was in Zion. God heard his prayers and answered him.

Zion is the place of unity in prayer.

> I was glad when they said unto me, Let us go into the house of the Lord. Our feet shall stand within thy gates, O Jerusalem. Jerusalem is builded as a city that is compact together: Whither the tribes go up, the tribes of the Lord, unto the testimony of Israel, to give thanks unto the name of the Lord.
>
> —Psalm 122:1–4

The tribes went up to Jerusalem. They went with gladness to the house of the Lord. We come to Zion with gladness. All the tribes of the earth are now welcome to come.

Jerusalem was the city that united the tribes. According to the *Bible Expository Commentary*, "When the psalmist looked at the city, he thought of unity and security. Just as the stones of the walls and houses were 'bound firmly together,' so the people were bound together in their worship of the Lord and their respect for the throne."[33]

They all had one place they were commanded to go to worship

and pray. Jerusalem was a city built for the multitudes. Zion is the assembly of God. Zion is the place of fellowship and unity.

Zion believers live in harmony and unity. We love the unity of the Spirit. Zion people have one heart and one mind. There is no division in Zion. Zion believers are of one accord and pray and worship together.

Zion is the place of the watchmen.

> I have set watchmen upon thy walls, O Jerusalem, which shall never hold their peace day nor night: ye that make mention of the LORD, keep not silence.
>
> —ISAIAH 62:6

The watchmen are the praying prophets, the seers. The watchmen see and pray. God sets the watchmen. Prayer ministries are found in Zion.

Here is another verse that connects Zion with watchmen.

> Thy watchmen shall lift up the voice; with the voice together shall they sing: for they shall see eye to eye, when the LORD shall bring again Zion.
>
> —ISAIAH 52:8

The watchmen prayed for the establishment and restoration of Zion. Zion is here because of prayer. You are Zion. You are here because of prayer. Those who loved Zion prayed for Zion.

MIGHT AND THE KINGDOM

Jesus and His disciples preached the arrival of the kingdom. The kingdom was coming in might to drive out and replace the kingdoms of darkness. This is why casting out demons was a sign of the kingdom's arrival (Matt. 12:28)

Might (power) is connected to the kingdom of God. The kingdom is preached and demonstrated. The kingdom is the rule and reign of the Holy Spirit in the hearts of men. Submitting to the rule of God in His kingdom is a key to walking in power and might:

> And lead us not into temptation, but deliver us from evil: For thine is the kingdom, and the power, and the glory, for ever. Amen.
>
> —MATTHEW 6:13

The kingdom is not just talk, but power.

> For the kingdom of God is not in word, but in power.
>
> —1 CORINTHIANS 4:20

When the kingdom comes, strength comes.

> And I heard a loud voice saying in heaven, Now is come salvation, and strength, and the kingdom of our God, and the power of his Christ.
>
> —REVELATION 12:10

Might is needed to advance the kingdom from generation to generation.

> They shall speak of the glory of thy kingdom, and talk of thy power; to make known to the sons of men his mighty acts, and the glorious majesty of his kingdom.
>
> —PSALM 145:11–12

> They will speak of the glory of your royal power and tell of your might.
>
> —PSALM 145:11, GNT

God's kingdom is a kingdom of glory and power. The kingdom is a place of mighty acts. We operate in and manifest the might of the King.

A PRAYER FOR MIGHT

Lord, You are the mighty God.

I receive the spirit of might.

Give me a revelation of Your might and power.

I will see and declare the mighty acts of the Lord.

Let miracles be released through Your might.

Let healing occur through Your might.

Let my words carry the spirit of might.

Let my prayers be mighty.

Let me walk in kingdom power and might.

Increase my wisdom and might.

I will wait on the Lord and renew my strength.

Let the Word of God be mighty in my life.

Lord, raise up mighty churches.

Let apostolic might be released in my region.

Let prophetic might be released in my region.

Let me be anointed for might.

Lord, release mighty prophetic words over my life.

Lord, let mighty prophetic utterances be released in my region.

Let me hear strong preaching.

Let me hear strong teaching.

Let the evangelists walk in might.

Let the pastors and teachers walk in might.

Let me be mighty in the Word.

Let me be mighty in revelation.

Let me be mighty in understanding.

STRENGTH AND MIGHT CONFESSIONS

I am strong in the Lord and in the power of His might.

I have the spirit of counsel and might.

I am strengthened by His Spirit in the inner man.

I have power to tread upon serpents and scorpions and over all the power of the enemy.

The Lord is the strength of my life.

The joy of the Lord is my strength.

I have wisdom, which gives me strength.

The Word of God is powerful and makes me strong.

I receive and walk in might and strength by faith.

Mighty God gives me strength.

The weapons of my warfare are not carnal but mighty through God to the pulling down of strongholds.

God has ordained strength out of my mouth.

The anointing gives me strength.

I will walk in strength all the days of my life.

The presence of God gives me strength.

In the Lord Jehovah is everlasting strength.

I go from strength to strength.

As my days are, so will be my strength.

Chapter 11

GOD'S MERCY TOWARD ZION

Thou shalt arise, and have mercy upon Zion: for the
time to favour her, yea, the set time, is come.
—PSALM 102:13

MERCY IS ANOTHER vital and important subject. Under-standing mercy will change your life. The Scriptures are filled with numerous references to the mercy of God. The Scriptures show the blessedness of those who receive and show mercy.

The Hebrew word for *mercy* is *checed* (*chesed*). This is another amazing word with a rich and deep meaning:

> The KJV translates Strong's H2617 in the following manner: mercy (149x), kindness (40x), lovingkindness (30x), good-ness (12x), kindly (5x), merciful (4x), favour (3x), good (1x), goodliness (1x), pity (1x), reproach (1x), wicked thing (1x).

> Hesed is kindness; by implication (toward God) piety; rarely (by opposition) reproof, or (subjectively) beauty:—favour, good deed(-liness, -ness), kindly, (loving-) kindness, merciful (kindness), mercy, pity, reproach, wicked thing. Mercy is God's kindness.[1]

Mercy is the opposite of wrath. God's wrath came on Jerusalem because of covenant violations, but God's mercy caused His favor to return. God's wrath was for a moment, but His kindness is everlasting (Isa. 54:8). God remembered His mercy in the time of wrath (Hab. 3:2).

God's kindness is upon Zion, and because you are Zion, God's kindness is also upon your life. Kindness is the quality of being friendly, generous, and considerate.[2] Synonyms for *kindness* include *kindheartedness, warmheartedness, affection, warmth, gentleness, concern, care, consideration, helpfulness, thoughtfulness, unselfishness, selflessness, compassion, sympathy, understanding, big-heartedness, benevolence, hospitality, generosity,* and *charitableness.*[3] This is God's attitude toward Zion. This is God's attitude toward you.

Hesed is also connected to covenant loyalty. God is loyal to Zion. God's loyalty and faithfulness to His covenant people have always been one of His outstanding attributes. His mercy (covenant loyalty) endures forever.

Zion is a place of mercy, compassion, and loving-kindness. God's mercy brings forgiveness, salvation, and deliverance. God's mercy is an extension of His goodness.

Psalm 136 is called the great *Hesed*.[4] Each verse says, "His mercy endures forever." The psalm describes God's great acts on behalf of His people. These acts were the result of His mercy. These acts include great wonders, the creation of the heaven and earth, the smiting of Egypt's firstborn, the overthrow of Pharaoh, the dividing of the Red Sea, and the smiting of famous kings. God does things for His people that He does not do for anyone else. This is the result of God's mercy.

> Do good in thy good pleasure unto Zion: build thou the walls of Jerusalem.
>
> —Psalm 51:18

Mercy is connected to goodness (Ps. 23:6). God does good in His good pleasure unto Zion. God does good things for Zion. God favors Zion with His goodness. The New International Version says, "May it please you to prosper Zion." God is gracious to Zion. God is benevolent to Zion. It pleases Him to rain prosperity over Zion.

...who redeemeth thy life from destruction; who crowneth thee with lovingkindness and tender mercies.

—Psalm 103:4

We are crowned with loving-kindness and tender mercies. He protects us from death and redeems us from the pit. The Voice translation says, "He crowns you with unfailing love and compassion like a king."

I want to emphasize the generous and benevolent aspect of God's mercy. God gives to all men liberally (Jas. 1:5). Our God is extremely generous. His generosity knows no bounds. God is generous to Zion. You are Zion. God is generous to you.

God does exceeding abundantly above all we can ask or think (Eph. 3:20). God gives us exceeding riches of grace (Eph. 1:19). God opens the windows (floodgates) of heaven and pours out more than we have room enough to receive (Mal. 3:10).

Zion is the place of God's abundance and generosity. God blesses His people abundantly in Zion. God overwhelms us with showers of blessing. He causes your cup to run over. This is all the result of His mercy.

But thou, O Lord, art a God full of compassion, and gracious, long suffering, and plenteous in mercy and truth. God is plenteous [abundant] in mercy.

—Psalm 86:15

He is abundant in kindness. God's kindness is abundant to Zion. You are Zion. You are a partaker of this abundant kindness and mercy. You are the recipient of abundant goodness.

God restored, delivered, chose, and favored Zion. God dwells in Zion. God blesses Zion. God put His glory on Zion. This was all the result of His mercy to Zion. This is why mercy is so important. We could not have any of these blessings apart from mercy.

Thou in thy mercy hast led forth the people which thou hast redeemed: thou hast guided them in thy strength unto thy holy habitation.

—Exodus 15:13

God, in His mercy, brought Israel out of Egypt. God, in His mercy, guided them to Zion, His holy habitation. Zion is the result of mercy. The people of Zion are the objects of God's mercy. You are Zion. You are the object of mercy and God's kindness.

The ark was the central piece of furniture in the tabernacle of Moses. The ark had upon it the mercy seat (Exod. 25:21). The mercy seat eventually came to Zion. Zion is the place of the mercy seat. The Lord promised to meet His people (specifically the high priest) at the mercy seat (Exod. 25:22). Christ is our mercy seat. God meets us in Zion. God's meets us with His mercy and kindness.

Blessed is he whose transgression is forgiven, whose sin is covered.

—Psalm 32:1

Blessed is the man to whom the Lord will not impute sin.

—Romans 4:8

The *mercy seat* means a "covering."[5] It was a lid that covered. Through Christ our sins are covered because He is our "covering." Zion is covered. You are covered. Your sins have been forgiven. You are blessed. This is all the result of mercy.

For the mountains shall depart, and the hills be removed; but my kindness shall not depart from thee, neither shall the covenant of my peace be removed, saith the Lord that hath mercy on thee.

—Isaiah 54:10

God's kindness will not depart from your life. Other translations say His faithfulness or faithful love will not depart. His love is steadfast and enduring. His covenant of peace (shalom) is with you. You are Zion. The Lord has mercy on you.

God's mercy on Zion is from generation to generation. His mercy is to a thousand generations (Deut. 7:9). God will always favor and be kind to Zion. We can trust and depend on the mercy of God. God's goodness to us will never end.

God magnifies His mercy (Gen. 19:19). Synonyms for *magnify* include *enlarge, maximize, increase, extend, expand, amplify,* and *intensity.*[6] To *magnify* means to make known or cause to be seen.[7] God magnifies His mercy upon your life. You are Zion. There is new mercy (kindness) on you. His mercy is increasing.

David received great mercy (1 Kings 3:6). This was a key to his victory and success. David made mistakes, but God's mercy was upon his life. The Scripture talks about the "sure mercies of David" (Isa. 55:3). God's mercies are sure (faithful and enduring).

> Great deliverance giveth he to his king; and sheweth mercy to his anointed, to David, and to his seed for evermore.
>
> —Psalm 18:50

Notice mercy is connected to great deliverance. God's mercy comes to His anointed. David was delivered from the plots and plans of the wicked. He defeated Saul. God preserved his life. He overcame the plot of Absalom. He overcame the betrayal of Ahithophel. He defeated Goliath and the Philistines. This was the result of mercy. You can overcome any plot of hell. God's mercy is upon your life. You are Zion.

The Amplified Bible translates Psalm 18:50 as "He gives great triumphs to His king." Victories come through mercy. Zion is a victorious city. Zion is the place of victory. You triumph in Christ (2 Cor. 2:14). You win victory after victory. God will not allow your enemies to triumph over you (Ps. 41:11).

> O praise the LORD, all ye nations: praise him, all ye people.
> For his merciful kindness is great toward us: and the truth of
> the LORD endureth for ever. Praise ye the LORD.
> —PSALM 117:1–2

Psalm 117 is the shortest psalm in the Bible. It is a psalm about God's merciful kindness. With just two verses and sixteen words in Hebrew, it is the shortest of all 150 psalms. It is the 595th of the 1,189 chapters of the King James Version of the Bible, making it the middle chapter. It is also the shortest chapter in this version of the Bible.[8] "O praise the LORD, all ye nations: praise him, all ye people." In other words, this psalm is in the center of the Bible. Mercy is in the heart of the book.

The nations are commanded to praise the Lord. In other words, the nations praise God because of His merciful kindness to Zion. Psalm 117:2 in the Amplified Bible says, "For His lovingkindness prevails over us [and we triumph and overcome through Him]."

> It is of the LORD's mercies that we are not consumed, because
> his compassions fail not.
> —LAMENTATIONS 3:22

Jeremiah wept over the destruction of Jerusalem. The curse had come to Jerusalem because of their covenant violations. Jerusalem became desolate and solitary. The enemy had destroyed her walls and gates. Death and famine ravaged the city.

They were not totally consumed because of God's mercy. His compassions failed not. Jeremiah remembered mercy in the midst of his weeping. Israel went into Babylon, but after seventy years they were released to come back to the city. Restoration followed judgment. Restoration is the result of mercy. You are Zion. You have been restored. His compassions do not fail. His mercies are new every morning (Lam. 3:23).

…which in time past were not a people, but are now the people of God: which had not obtained mercy, but now have obtained mercy.

—1 Peter 2:10

We are now the people of God. We who had not obtained mercy, have now received mercy. Zion is a people. Zion people are people of mercy. God's mercy is known and celebrated in Zion. We sing of the mercy of God (Ps. 101:1).

God's mercy brought the nations to Zion. God had mercy on Zion, and God had mercy on the people of the earth. Every nation has experienced this mercy. His mercy extends to the uttermost part of the earth. There is no place where His mercy has not come.

God is not angry with you. His anger is turned away from Zion (Isa. 12:1). God has comforted Zion. You are Zion. You have been comforted. The prophet was told to speak comfortably to Jerusalem (Isa. 40:1–2). Isaiah 49:13 says,

Sing, O heavens; and be joyful, O earth; and break forth into singing, O mountains: for the LORD hath comforted his people, and will have mercy upon his afflicted.

Mercy and comfort are joined together. *Comfort* is defined as the easing or alleviation of a person's feelings of grief or distress.[9] Zion is the place of comfort. Zion is the place of consolation. You are Zion. You have been comforted. God increases your greatness and comforts you on every side (Ps. 71:21).

For the LORD shall comfort Zion: he will comfort all her waste places; and he will make her wilderness like Eden, and her desert like the garden of the LORD; joy and gladness shall be found therein, thanksgiving, and the voice of melody.

—Isaiah 51:3

God comforts our waste places and make our wilderness like an Eden. Your desert places will become like the garden of the Lord. God waters our dry places. He releases streams in the desert. Zion is a watered place. You are Zion. You are watered. You are the garden of the Lord.

> Therefore they shall come and sing in the height of Zion, and shall flow together to the goodness of the LORD, for wheat, and for wine, and for oil, and for the young of the flock and of the herd: and their soul shall be as a watered garden; and they shall not sorrow any more at all.
>
> —JEREMIAH 31:12

Zion has wheat, wine, and oil. This is another picture of prosperity and abundance. Zion is like a watered garden. This is a picture of the goodness of the Lord. You are Zion. You are a watered garden. There is no famine in your land.

The Contemporary English Version says that Zion "will be prosperous and grow like a garden with plenty of water." Do you see yourself as a well-watered garden? This is how God sees you. You are Zion. You are prosperous. Your dry places are now irrigated. Jeremiah 17:8 says, "For he shall be as a tree planted by the waters, and that spreadeth out her roots by the river, and shall not see when heat cometh, but her leaf shall be green; and shall not be careful in the year of drought, neither shall cease from yielding fruit."

Chapter 12

I AM ZION, HOLY
AND SOUGHT OUT!

And they shall call them, The holy people, The redeemed of the
LORD: and thou shalt be called, Sought out, A city not forsaken.
—ISAIAH 62:12

ECEIVED THE FOLLOWING word while preaching at a prophetic
gathering in Killeen, Texas. It is a word of turnaround for those
who read this book. I was preaching about the Lord giving people
a new name. A new name represents a new identity, a new season,
and a new life:

> Declaring, "I am Zion!" is your claim to this new and spiri-
> tual identity that God has already assigned to you. When
> you declare, "I am Zion," you are positioning yourself for a
> new season and a new life. As you claim your Zion identity,
> get ready to be sought out. Get ready for people to gather to
> you. Get ready for them to come to you from distant places.
> Get ready for new favor and new prosperity to come to your
> life. Zion is a city that is sought out. You are Zion. You are
> sought out.

As this word came to me, two verses from Isaiah chapter 62 also
came to me. The first one:

> And the Gentiles shall see thy righteousness, and all kings
> thy glory: and thou shalt be called by a new name, which the
> mouth of the LORD shall name.
>
> —ISAIAH 62:2

The second one reads:

> And they shall call them, The holy people, The redeemed of
> the LORD: and thou shalt be called, Sought out, A city not
> forsaken.
> —Isaiah 62:12

The International Children's Bible says verse 12 like this: "His
people will be called the Holy People. They will be called the
Saved People of the Lord. And Jerusalem will be called the City
God Wants. It will be named the City God Has Not Rejected."

God gives us a new name, and that name is Sought Out.

Sought out is a powerful word of restoration. It is a word that
signifies favor and blessing. It is a word that brings about change. It
is a word that releases a new season.

WHAT'S IN A NAME?

What is the significance of this new name and who receives it? In
context it was a promise given to Israel. Israel had suffered desolation as a result of covenant violations. Israel's condition is described
by Jeremiah in Lamentations.

> How doth the city sit solitary, that was full of people!
> how is she become as a widow! she that was great among
> the nations, and princess among the provinces, how is she
> become tributary!
> —Lamentations 1:1

Israel had become solitary, her people dispersed to Babylon. No
one would come to her. Instead of joy and blessing, there was be
weeping and sorrow. Yet Isaiah was prophesying their restoration
and glory through Messiah. There would be a divine turnaround.
They would go from being desolate and empty to being sought out.

The prophecy is also the same for us as Zion, the city of God.
Zion is a sought-out city, the mountain of God. It is also the
church. People will seek out the church. They come to the church

to be taught and to learn the ways of the Lord. The church will not be empty but filled with people.

> And many people shall go and say, Come ye, and let us go up to the mountain of the LORD, to the house of the God of Jacob; and he will teach us of his ways, and we will walk in his paths: for out of Zion shall go forth the law, and the word of the LORD from Jerusalem.
> —ISAIAH 2:3

The prophet Zechariah saw Zion filled with the young and the old. Multitudes will come to Zion.

> Thus saith the LORD of hosts; There shall yet old men and old women dwell in the streets of Jerusalem, and every man with his staff in his hand for very age. And the streets of the city shall be full of boys and girls playing in the streets thereof.
> —ZECHARIAH 8:4–5

Promotion and favor are available to people of all ages. The move of God is not for one generation but for all generations. This includes you! God wants to bring a move of glory to your life that will access uncommon levels of favor and promotion.

A single encounter with the glory can launch you in an entirely new direction. As we've discovered, the glory expands and enlarges. The glory invades and encounters. The glory releases and reveals.

Let's look at a few of the many examples in Scripture of being sought out.

SOLOMON WAS SOUGHT OUT

The queen of Sheba sought out Solomon. She came from the ends of the earth to hear his wisdom.

> And when the queen of Sheba heard of the fame of Solomon concerning the name of the LORD, she came to prove him with hard questions. And she came to Jerusalem with a very great train, with camels that bare spices, and very much gold,

and precious stones: and when she was come to Solomon, she communed with him of all that was in her heart. And Solomon told her all her questions: there was not any thing hid from the king, which he told her not.

—1 Kings 10:1–3

The queen of Sheba came with gold and precious stones. Glory attracts wealth and prominent people. There is deliverance from lack and defeat in the glory. As the glory hits your life, wealth will also hit your life! The church has suffered for far too long because it rejected the supernatural power of increase in the glory.

And she gave the king an hundred and twenty talents of gold, and of spices very great store, and precious stones: there came no more such abundance of spices as these which the queen of Sheba gave to king Solomon.

—1 Kings 10:10

The queen of Sheba blessed Solomon with an abundance of gifts. Solomon also blessed Sheba. She sought him out and received the desire of her heart. Solomon answered her hard questions. People will seek you out because they have questions that need answers.

THE PROPHETS AND APOSTLES WERE SOUGHT OUT

God has imparted great power and anointing upon His servants. Throughout history both prophets and apostles have been instrumental in ministering the glory of God in the earth. From prophetic words of favor and warning to miracles of healing and deliverance, they are sought out as holy men and women of God.

Huldah

During the reign of King Josiah, Israel underwent a great revival. The king had ordered the destruction of all idols and traces of idol worship throughout the land. As the people went out to obey the king, Shaphan the scribe and Hilkiah the priest came upon "a book of the law of the Lord given by Moses" (2 Chron. 34:14). Because the people had been so far from God for so long, they didn't know what to do with the book. When King Josiah became aware of the discovery, he commanded the priest and the scribe to go and inquire of the Lord concerning the book and what it meant (v. 21).

There was only one person in Judah whom the two men knew to turn to, one who they knew could hear from God and interpret the words in the book—Huldah, the prophetess:

> And Hilkiah, and they that the king had appointed, went to Huldah the prophetess, the wife of Shallum the son of Tikvath, the son of Hasrah, keeper of the wardrobe; (now she dwelt in Jerusalem in the college:) and they spake to her to that effect. And she answered them, Thus saith the LORD God of Israel.
> —2 CHRONICLES 34:22–23

This account is repeated in 2 Kings 22, but within this story is the only time we see Huldah mentioned. She was sought out at a critical time in Israel's history, and she had the ears to hear God.

Israel experienced a great turnaround under Josiah's leadership, and it was because the glory and favor of God rested on this woman prophet who could deliver the word of the Lord in a critical hour.

Elisha

In 2 Kings 5:1–16 Naaman the leper sought out Elisha and was healed from leprosy. In the Old Testament, prophets were often sought out for direction and healing. Hunger and pursuit unlock vital prophetic anointing.

Joseph

Joseph was sought out to interpret Pharaoh's dream. He went from prison to the palace. His gift made room for him. He was promoted in the kingdom as a result. Gifts are lying dormant in your belly that will cause you to be sought out! Stir them up and be faithful to grow in them.

> Then Pharaoh sent and called Joseph, and they brought him hastily out of the dungeon: and he shaved himself,

and changed his raiment, and came in unto Pharaoh. And Pharaoh said unto Joseph, I have dreamed a dream, and there is none that can interpret it: and I have heard say of thee, that thou canst understand a dream to interpret it.

And Joseph answered Pharaoh, saying, It is not in me: God shall give Pharaoh an answer of peace.

—Genesis 41:14–16

Daniel

Daniel was also sought out to interpret dreams. He interpreted the king's dream when no one else could. What gifts do you have? What talents and abilities do you possess? People in need will seek you out.

O Belteshazzar, master of the magicians, because I know, that the spirit of the holy gods is in thee, and no secret troubleth thee, tell me the visions of my dream that I have seen, and the interpretation thereof.

—Daniel 4:9

David

David was sought out for his musical ability. He came to Saul to refresh him when he came under the influence of an evil spirit.

And Saul said unto his servants, Provide me now a man that can play well, and bring him to me. Then answered one of the servants, and said, Behold, I have seen a son of Jesse the Bethlehemite, that is cunning in playing, and a mighty valiant man, and a man of war, and prudent in matters, and a comely person, and the Lord is with him. Wherefore Saul sent messengers unto Jesse, and said, Send me David thy son, which is with the sheep.

—1 Samuel 16:17–19

Those who are skillful will be sought out. What skills do you have that will cause people to seek you out?

Apostles

The apostles were sought out. Multitudes came to be healed:

> And believers were the more added to the Lord, multitudes
> both of men and women. Insomuch that they brought forth
> the sick into the streets, and laid them on beds and couches,
> that at the least the shadow of Peter passing by might over-
> shadow some of them. There came also a multitude out of
> the cities round about unto Jerusalem, bringing sick folks,
> and them which were vexed with unclean spirits: and they
> were healed every one.
>
> —ACTS 5:14–16

Cornelius was told by an angel to seek out Peter. (See Acts 10.)
Peter came to his house and preached, and his entire family was
saved and Spirit-filled.

JESUS WAS SOUGHT OUT

Jesus was always sought out. The multitudes sought Him out for
teaching, healing, and deliverance.

> And there followed him great multitudes of people from
> Galilee, and from Decapolis, and from Jerusalem, and from
> Judaea, and from beyond Jordan.
>
> —MATTHEW 4:25

Jesus was sought out by the wise men at His birth (Matt. 2:1–12).
Jesus was sought out by Nicodemus who came by night (John 3:2).
Jesus was sought out by a woman of Canaan for deliverance of her
daughter (Matt. 15:22). Many sought Jesus as they came to the
feasts in Jerusalem. They came to Jerusalem to see Him and hear
His teaching.

> Then sought they for Jesus, and spake among themselves, as
> they stood in the temple, What think ye, that he will not
> come to the feast?
>
> —JOHN 11:56

The Greeks also sought after Jesus.

> And there were certain Greeks among them that came up
> to worship at the feast: The same came therefore to Philip,
> which was of Bethsaida of Galilee, and desired him, saying,
> Sir, we would see Jesus.
>
> —John 12:20–21

This is a picture of strangers and foreigners coming to seek you out.

You Will Be Sought Out

Not only is Isaiah chapter 60 the glory chapter, but it is also a prophecy that shows us what happens when we are sought out. The results are amazing and wonderful.

> Arise, shine; for thy light is come, and the glory of the LORD
> is risen upon thee. For, behold, the darkness shall cover the
> earth, and gross darkness the people: but the LORD shall
> arise upon thee, and his glory shall be seen upon thee. And
> the Gentiles shall come to thy light, and kings to the bright-
> ness of thy rising.
>
> —Isaiah 60:1–3

People are drawn to light. They come because of light and glory. You are sought out when there is light and glory in your life.

It is time for you to arise and shine. Arise from a low place and come up to a high place. This is a picture of promotion. The glory of God has been given to the church.

This light and glory shine in darkness. Those living in darkness come to those who have light. God wants you to shine with His glory. This is why you will be sought out. Glory becomes a magnet that attracts people to you. They are attracted to your ministry, your business, and your calling and gifting. They are attracted to the blessing upon your life.

> Lift up thine eyes round about, and see: all they gather them-
> selves together, they come to thee: thy sons shall come from
> far, and thy daughters shall be nursed at thy side. Then thou

shalt see, and flow together, and thine heart shall fear, and be enlarged; because the abundance of the sea shall be converted unto thee, the forces of the Gentiles shall come unto thee.

—Isaiah 60:4–5

Isaiah prophesies about the sons and daughters coming to you. This is a picture of great blessing. Sons and daughters have always been a sign of blessing and productivity. They gather to you.

Churches and ministries that are sought out will attract many sons and daughters. They come to be nurtured. They come to be taught. They come to be trained and released. They come to be nursed at your side. Isaiah prophesied extensively about the sons and daughters coming.

I will say to the north, Give up; and to the south, Keep not back: bring my sons from far, and my daughters from the ends of the earth.

—Isaiah 43:6

Thus saith the Lord God, Behold, I will lift up mine hand to the Gentiles, and set up my standard to the people: and they shall bring thy sons in their arms, and thy daughters shall be carried upon their shoulders.

—Isaiah 49:22

And strangers shall stand and feed your flocks, and the sons of the alien shall be your plowmen and your vinedressers.

—Isaiah 61:5

Where are the sons and daughters? Are they gathering to you? Are you being sought out?

That our sons may be as plants grown up in their youth; that our daughters may be as corner stones, polished after the similitude of a palace.

—Psalm 144:12

Places of glory won't have to plead. People will be supernaturally drawn. The atmosphere of heaven will go forth like a magnet in the spirit and cause people to come forth. This is the effect of the glory on a ministry. Hungry people come, and uncommon results break forth.

Ministries with glory raise up sons and daughters who help establish the vision and mandate of the house. Far too many are laboring with little or no results. They are toiling without the glory. I feel a strong call in my spirit for the church to return to the glory. This is a time and season of redefinition. God is redefining and aligning people and ministries in His glory. The glory is the mandate of the hour.

As the glory of the Lord arises, sons and daughters will take their places. If your ministry is barren, without authentic sons and daughters, you may need to get back to the glory. You may need to dig some old wells again or strike the ground to break open new ones. When you get the glory manifesting, you will see an increase. Sons and daughters will surround you to worship with you, build with you and advance with you. You will go from pleading to being sought out.

I am praying that God will raise up sought-out places of glory, sought-out places of healing and delivering power, sought-out places of family and love, sought-out places of mercy and forgiveness, and sought-out places of power and advancement.

GET WISDOM AND FAVOR, AND BE SOUGHT OUT

Wisdom opens the doorway! You cannot walk in the wisdom of God and not be sought out. You need to daily decree and declare divine wisdom over your life. As you spend quality time with God, His mind will come forth in your life. His wisdom is pouring out. You will do things you never thought you could do. You will go places you never thought you would go. He is rewriting your story in His glory.

Like Solomon, as you grow in the wisdom of God, you will be sought out, just as he was:

> And king Solomon gave to the queen of Sheba all her desire, whatsoever she asked, beside that which she had brought unto the king. So she turned, and went away to her own land, she and her servants.
>
> —2 Chronicles 9:12

And king Solomon gave unto the queen of Sheba all her
desire, whatsoever she asked, beside that which Solomon
gave her of his royal bounty. So she turned and went to her
own country, she and her servants.

—1 KINGS 10:13

As Solomon gave the queen of Sheba gifts from his royal bounty,
you will deposit something of value into the lives of those who seek
you out, and they will be blessed. People will be blessed when they
seek you out.

Surely the isles shall wait for me, and the ships of Tarshish
first, to bring thy sons from far, their silver and their gold
with them, unto the name of the LORD thy God, and to the
Holy One of Israel, because he hath glorified thee. And the
sons of strangers shall build up thy walls, and their kings
shall minister unto thee: for in my wrath I smote thee, but
in my favour have I had mercy on thee.

—ISAIAH 60:9–10

The sons come with silver and gold. This is a picture of prosperity coming to those who are sought out. Strangers also come to
build the walls and minister to you. We discussed this in chapter
8. Isaiah then speaks about favor. An increase of glory releases an
increase of favor. Favor attracts people to your life. Favor causes
people to seek you out. Strangers and foreigners show up.

OPEN GATES BRING WEALTH TO THE SOUGHT OUT

Therefore thy gates shall be open continually; they shall not
be shut day nor night; that men may bring unto thee the
forces of the Gentiles, and that their kings may be brought.

—ISAIAH 60:11

Gates represent access. Men bring wealth through these gates.
They seek out Zion and bring their wealth into it. John saw these
gates open in the Book of Revelation.

> And the gates of it shall not be shut at all by day: for there
> shall be no night there.
>
> —Revelation 21:25

The gates are never shut. Those who are sought out constantly attract wealth. Prosperity comes to those who are sought out.

Isaiah and John saw pictures of the kingdom and those entering the kingdom. Zion is a wealthy place, a wealthy city. We should expect to be sought out. This is what God calls us. This is our identity. This is who we are.

From Hated and Afflicted to Sought Out

> The sons also of them that afflicted thee shall come bending
> unto thee; and all they that despised thee shall bow them-
> selves down at the soles of thy feet; and they shall call thee;
> The city of the Lord, The Zion of the Holy One of Israel.
>
> —Isaiah 60:14

Even those who hated and afflicted you will seek you out to submit to you. This is God's restorative promise to Zion. This is His promise to you.

This is a great word because many times in our journey we go through difficult times of persecution. Sometimes we just want to pack it all up and retreat, but God has a way of turning it all around. The very people whom the enemy used to attack and berate you can become a part of your increase, as long as you stay planted in the will of the Father.

> Whereas thou has been forsaken and hated, so that no man
> went through thee, I will make thee an eternal excellency, a
> joy of many generations.
>
> —Isaiah 60:15

The opposite of being sought out is being hated and forsaken. Have you ever felt hated and forsaken? Have you suffered from rejection and isolation? Many have been in a place of loneliness and defeat.

The good news is that through His covenant of peace, salvation, and deliverance, He is giving you a new name in Zion: Sought out.

As Zion you should expect to be sought out. You are no longer despised. You are no longer rejected. You are no longer overlooked. You are no longer desolate. You are the dwelling place of God.

People are drawn to you for salvation, deliverance, and healing. They come to be taught. They come to hear the Word of the Lord. They come to receive counsel and wisdom. In return they bring wealth. They bring honor. They come to serve. They come to worship the King. This is the kingdom. This is restoration. This is the result of the glory of God.

Multiplied blessings are coming to you. Believe it. Confess it. Meditate on these scriptures. Receive the word of the Lord: you are Zion, and you are sought out.

SOUGHT-OUT CONFESSIONS

I am Zion.

I will arise and shine for my light has come, and the glory of the Lord has risen upon me.

His light shall be seen upon my life by those in darkness.

I am sought out.

I am not rejected, overlooked, or desolate, but I am sought out. Sons and daughters come to me because I am sought out. Strangers seek me out. Even my haters will come and submit.

My gates are always open for blessings to come into my life.

Favor is upon my life because of the glory of God. Favor is opening the right doors for me at the right time.

God is adding the right people to me and removing the wrong ones. I am a part of Zion, the city of the Lord, which is sought out. Zion is filled with people because it is a city sought out.

My steps are ordered of the Lord.

I live in sync with heaven's plan for my life. My ministry is sought out.

I am walking in new levels and receiving uncommon revelation and direction for my life.

Expansion is manifesting.

Kings and prominent people come to me because I am sought out.

The camels are coming to me. Caravans of blessing are coming my way.

Wealth comes to me because I am sought out.

Increase comes to me because I am sought out.

Streams of income and increase are coming forth in my life.

I enjoy abundance because I am sought out.

Multiplication comes into my life because I am sought out.

I receive upgrades in every area of my life because I am sought out.

I experience riches, blessings, and glory in my life because I am sought out.

> Lord, I come to You right now, and I receive this prophetic word that I am sought out. I am not lost, but I am found. You said You came to seek and save me. I have fully surrendered my life to You; therefore, barrenness has no place in my life.
>
> I repent of limited thinking and believing. I repent for not fully embracing Your promise and potential for my life. I have heard, read, and received this word from heaven that I am sought out.
>
> I will walk forth in the power of this word! I break all limitation off my life, and I loose the unlimited power and blessings of heaven over me. I decree I am no longer desolate, but I am sought out, in Jesus' name. Amen.

PROPHETIC POEMS OF ZION

A Heavenly Kingdom

The kingdom without observation,
Not what the Pharisees were looking for,
A spiritual kingdom for spiritual people,
Those born again would enter the door.

The natural man cannot understand it,
Nicodemus was perplexed,
He asked a question of the Lord,
Do you go back into the womb again?

They were looking for an earthly kingdom,
They were waiting for an earthly king,
Jesus did not come to give them either,
A heavenly kingdom He would bring.

The kingdom was at hand,
It took discernment to see,
Demons were being cast out,
The captives were being set free.

The kingdom was arriving in power,
Heal the sick and raise the dead,
He sent the twelve to preach it,
And demonstrate what was said.

The rule of God had arrived,
The demons knew it well,
They submitted to heaven's authority,
They fled, and their kingdom fell.

The justice of God had arrived,
The days of vengeance had come,
The blood of the prophets avenged,
The will of God would be done.

A new covenant would arrive,
The old had become obsolete,
A new people would be formed,
The old rulers He would unseat.

Many would oppose the kingdom,
They would fight the heavenly King,
He that sat in the heaven would laugh,
The son of David would take His seat.

The kingdom would advance,
Its increase would have no end,
From generation to generation,
In the church, world without end.

THOUSANDS

Moses prayed and blessed Israel,
He prayed they would multiply by thousands,
Rebekah was blessed,
To be the mother of thousands of millions.

Saul killed his thousands,
David killed his ten thousands,
Saul became jealous of the song,
And began to chase David with thousands.

David was not afraid of ten thousands,
That gathered against him round about,
God delivered him from thousands,
He delivered him from the jealous Saul.

Samson killed a thousand,
With the jawbone of an ass,
May God give you victory over your thousands,
For one can chase a thousand.

Thousands of angels in the heavenly army,
Ten thousand times ten thousand they are,
There are more that be for us than against us,
They will help us win the battles that come.

A thousand will fall at thy side,
Ten thousand at thy right hand,
This is the promise of God,
It will not come nigh thee.

David gave thousands to the temple,
Solomon offered a thousand burnt offerings,
Kings gave in the thousands,
Offerings in the thousands can be released.

May your sheep bring forth thousands,
And may you bring forth ten thousands—
This is the blessing of the Lord;
This is your harvest.

Solomon spoke thousands of proverbs,
He wrote over a thousand songs,
The thousand women were his downfall.
One thousand wives and concubines in all.

Jesus fed five thousand,
With a few fish and loaves,
The miracle of multiplication,
Thousands came forth with His blessing.

Three thousand were saved at Pentecost,
Five thousand added to the church later,
This is the power of Pentecost,
Thousands are the result of miracles.

Ruling and reigning with Christ a thousand years,
Satan bound a thousand years,
The kingdom of God represented by thousands,
The city of God twelve thousand furlongs long.

Ezekiel saw a river measured by a thousand cubits.
One thousand to the ankles,
One thousand to the loins,
One thousand to the shoulders.

Jesus is one among a thousand,
He stands out among the thousands,
There is no one as beautiful as He,
He is the chiefest among ten thousand.

THE WILLOWS (PSALM 137)

They hung their harps upon the willows,
In Babylon, they wept,
They could not sing in a strange land.

For seventy years they remained,
In captivity, they stayed,
Away from Jerusalem their city.

But then deliverance came,
King Cyrus issued the decree,
They were able to leave Babylon,
And return to Jerusalem free.

They took their harps from the willows,
They began to sing again,
Their joy returned to them,
The played music once again.

Take your harps from the willows,
It is time for you to do it again,
Pick up your gift once more,
Deliverance has come this day.

Take your gift from the willow tree,
Let it no longer hang there,
Stir up the gift inside of you,
Use it to bless again.

The days of sadness are over,
God has dried your tears,
The joy of the Lord has returned,
Your deliverance is near.

It's time to write again,
It's time to dance again,
It's time to sing again,
It's time to preach again.

Take your gift down from the willow tree,
It does not belong there anymore,
The day of restoration has come,
It will not hang there anymore.

THE GLORY REALM

I have called you to the glory realm,
The realm of power,
The realm of favor,
The realm of abundance.

I have called you to the glory realm,
The realm of holiness,
The realm of beauty,
The realm of no limits.

I have called you to the glory realm,
The realm of riches,
The realm of prosperity,
The realm of gold and silver.

I have called you to the glory realm,
The realm of majesty,
The realm of splendor,
The realm where nothing is impossible.

I have called you to the glory realm,
The realm of promotion,
The realm of elevation,
The realm where you arise.

I called you to the glory realm,
The realm of revelation,
The realm of insight,
The realm of wisdom.

I have called you to the glory realm,
The realm of open gates,
The realm of blessing,
The realm of increase and enlargement.

I have called you to the glory realm,
The realm of peace,
The realm of safety,
The realm of no fear.

I have called you to the glory realm,
The realm of salvation,
The realm of praise,
The realm of worship.

I have called you to the glory realm,
The realm of upgrade,
The realm of thousands,
The realm multiplication.

I have called you to the glory realm,
The realm of shouting,
The realm of dancing,
The realm of eternal joy.

I have called you to the glory realm,
The realm of love,
The realm of hope,
The realm of faith.

Walk in this realm,
Live in this realm,
Abide in this realm,
This is the place for you.

This is Zion,
This is the mountain,
This is the river,
This is My kingdom.

This is the place of My presence,
This is the place of My weight,
This is the place of My fame,
The place of My rain.

My angels are here,
The seraphim are here,
The cherubim are here,
The elders bow here.

This is the place of thunder,
This is the place of lightning,
This is the place fire,
This is the Holy Place.

THE ENLARGED TENT OF ISRAEL (ISAIAH 54:2)

"Enlarge your tent and stretch forth your curtains,
You will break out on the right hand and on the left."
Isaiah spoke this to Israel,
That the nations were coming.

The Tent of Israel was not large enough to receive them,
The Gentiles were coming in,
A new tent God would raise up,
The church would be the place.

On the Day of Pentecost,
The new tent began to form,
Thousands came into it,
And a new community was born.

Ten years after Pentecost Cornelius heard the call,
Peter went to his house and preached,
The Holy Spirit began to fall,
On the Gentiles came the mercy of God.

The multitudes began to come into this tent,
To the Gentiles, the apostle Paul was sent,
Many nations heard the Word,
They came into the church to seek.

This tent expanded throughout the world,
There is no limit to who can come,
This tent is here today,
The church is that enlarged place.

This tent is large enough to house your city,
This tent can house a nation,
There is plenty of room for souls to enter,
The Lord has made the space.

Let us believe for the multitudes to come in,
Let revival come to our land,
Multitudes are coming to this tent,
They are being brought in by the Lord's hand.

THE GLORY REALM IS THE MEGA REALM

The realm of righteousness,
The realm of multiplication,
The realm of abundance.

The realm of thousands,
The realm of millions,
And the realm of billions—
This is the unlimited realm.

The realm of immensity,
The realm of endless expansion,
And the realm of unlimited growth—
This is the kingdom realm.

There is mega grace,
There is mega favor,
And there is mega power—
This is the glory realm.

There are mega miracles,
There are mega healings,
And there is mega deliverance—
This is the glory realm.

The realm of light,
The realm of revelation,
And the realm of wisdom—
This is the glory realm.

The realm of peace,
The realm of prosperity,
And the realm of gladness—
This is the realm of shalom.

Enter into this realm,
And you will break free
From the limitations
That are holding thee.

Breakthroughs are yours;
They come in abundance,
And nothing can hold you back—
This is the glory realm.

It is a large place,
It is a wealthy place,
And there is no lack—
This is the glory realm.

GIVER

Spare not in your giving,
Do not hold back,
It the key to breakthrough,
It is the key to blessing.

God spared not His Son,
He gave Him to us freely,
He will give us all things,
And that more abundantly.

He that sows sparingly,
Shall reap sparingly,
He that sows abundantly,
Shall reap abundantly.

Spare not in your giving,
Lengthen thy cords,
Strengthen thy stakes,
Break out of the place of limitation.

Do not spare because of fear,
Do not spare because of unbelief,
Do not spare in your giving,
It is the season of breakthrough.

THE ASAPHS ARE ARISING

When David brought the ark,
From Obed-Edom's house,
He set it under a tent,
In the mountain of the Lord.

He called for the families of Asaph,
And the families of Heman and Jeduthun,
To come and worship before the ark,
To sing and prophesy with instruments.

There is a new generation,
Of Asaphs arising in the earth,
They are the descendants of Asaph,
The seer appointed to worship.

These are spiritual descendants,
Not descendants after the flesh,
But those who worship in the Spirit,
Spiritual sons and daughters.

The family of Asaph,
Stood before the ark continually,
Singing the songs of the Lord,
Prophesying with the instruments.

Asaph's name means to gather,
We gather to worship today,
We gather in His presence,
We prophesy in His glory.

The sons of Asaph continued,
To minister for generations,
They were faithful to sing and play,
They carried the mantle of worship.

Sometimes they were hidden,
In times of rebellion and sin,
But they would always come forth,
In times of restoration.

They were seen in Hezekiah's day,
They were seen in Josiah's day,
They were seen in Nehemiah's day,
They are being seen today.

Are you an Asaph?
Will you continue what was established
Years ago by king David?

HERE AND ADVANCING

Some believe things are getting worse,
Some believe things are getting better,
Your worldview determines which,
The lens through which you see.

Some say the kingdom is coming,
Some believe the kingdom is here,
Some it is now but not yet,
This will affect your worldview.

The way you look at the world,
The way you see the future,
It all comes through a lens,
Whether it is getting better or worse.

The kingdom is advancing,
Its increase will have no end,
This is what Isaiah saw,
From generation to generation.

If the kingdom is not here now,
Then things will get worse,
If the kingdom is here and advancing,
Then things will get better.

Your worldview as a believer,
Depends on what you are taught,
Make no mistake about it,
Your teaching means a lot.

GLORY ENCOUNTER

A glory encounter will change you,
A glory encounter is what you need,
A glory encounter with the living God,
The God of glory wants to meet with you.

Moses encountered His glory,
To the holy Mountain, he went,
His face shined with the glory,
He hid his face from the people he was sent.

Solomon encountered the glory,
He and the priests sacrificed,
The cloud filled the temple,
They could not stand it was so thick,

Isaiah saw the glory,
In the temple, it was revealed,
He heard the cry of "Holy, Holy, Holy,"
To the nation, he was sent.

The disciples saw the glory,
On the mount of transfiguration,
They beheld the brightness,
When the Lord on the mountain prayed.

The glory fell on Pentecost,
It came like a mighty wind,
Cloven tongues of fire sat on them.
In other languages, they began to speak.

Saul encountered the glory,
He encountered the risen Lord,
A light shined from heaven,
He fell at the feet of the Lord.

John saw His glory,
On the island of Patmos, he did see,
The Glory of the risen Lord,
He heard the cry, "Holy, Holy, Holy."

An encounter with the glory will change you,
You cannot stay the same,
Your life will be transformed,
When you see His glory and His fame.

NOTES

Introduction: A Chosen Place for a Chosen People

1.   Steve Rudd, "Babylonian Talmud: Ancient Synagogue Literary Sources," Interactive Bible, accessed September 12, 2019, http://www.bible.ca/synagogues/Ancient-Synagogue-Archeological-Literary-Sources-Bible-Jesus-Israel-Judea-diaspora-first-century-oldest-pre70AD-Babylonian-Talmud-Non-Biblical-Jewish-Law-500ad.htm.

2.   "What Is Zion?" Got Questions, accessed September 12, 2019, https://www.gotquestions.org/Zion.html.

3.   "What Is Zion?" Got Questions.

Chapter 1: The Stronghold of Zion

1.   Blue Letter Bible, s.v. "*armown*," accessed September 12, 2019, https://www.blueletterbible.org/lang/lexicon/lexicon.cfm?Strongs=H759&t=KJV.

2.   *Merriam-Webster*, s.v. "fortify," accessed September 12, 2019, https://www.merriam-webster.com/dictionary/fortify.

3.   *Merriam-Webster*, s.v. "bulwark," accessed September 12, 2019, https://www.merriam-webster.com/dictionary/bulwark.

Chapter 2: The Habitation of God

1.   Bible Hub, "Psalm 122:4." accessed September 26, 2019, https://biblehub.com/commentaries/psalms/122-4.htm.

2.   Hanko Cornelius, "Jonah's Preaching to Nineveh," Standard Bearer, accessed September 16, 2019, https://standardbearer.rfpa.org/node/43021.

3.   "The Southern Kingdom of Judah," Bible History, accessed September 23, 2019, https://www.bible-history.com/old-testament/judah.html.

4.   Blue Letter Bible, s.v. "*ad*," accessed September 25, 2019, https://www.blueletterbible.org/lang/lexicon/lexicon.cfm?Strongs=H5703&t=KJV.

5.   Blue Letter Bible, s.v. "*owlam*," accessed September 25, 2019, https://www.blueletterbible.org/lang/lexicon/lexicon.cfm?Strongs=H5769&t=KJV.

6.   Lance Wallnau, ""Strange but true - It's a voice-activated universe," Facebook, July 3, 2018, https://www.facebook.com/LanceWallnau/photos/a.178800949935/10156553167569936/?type=3&theater.

Chapter 3: Born of Zion

1. Hedley Palmer, "Psalm 87: Zion City of Our God," ICLnet, 1996, http://www.iclnet.org/pub/resources/text/hpalmer/psalms/ps-087.txt.

2. Blue Letter Bible, "Messiah," accessed September 17, 2019, https://www.blueletterbible.org/search/search.cfm?Criteria=messiah&t=KJV#s=s_primary_0_1.

3. Blue Letter Bible, s.v. "*mashiyach*," accessed September 17, 2019, https://www.blueletterbible.org/lang/lexicon/lexicon.cfm?Strongs=H4899&t=KJV.

4. *Merriam-Webster*, s.v. "scepter," accessed September 18, 2019, https://www.merriam-webster.com/dictionary/scepter.

5. *Merriam-Webster*, s.v. "mountain," accessed September 23, 2019, https://www.merriam-webster.com/dictionary/mountain.

Chapter 4: The River of God

1. "2016: Todd Dennis—Preterist Idealism, A Hermeneutic for Today," The Preterist Archive, accessed September 19, 2019, https://www.preteristarchive.com/Idealism/2006_dennis_jerusalem-heart.html.

2. Reinhard Bonnke, "A Swimming Lesson From Ezekiel," Christ for All Nations, accessed September 19, 2019, https://www.cfan.eu/resources/bible-studies/detail-bible-study/a-swimming-lesson-from-ezekiel/.

3. Blue Letter Bible, s.v. "*massa*," accessed September 19, 2019, https://www.blueletterbible.org/lang/lexicon/lexicon.cfm?t=kjv&strongs=h4853.

4. Blue Letter Bible, s.v. "*mayan*," accessed September 19, 2019, https://www.blueletterbible.org/lang/lexicon/lexicon.cfm?Strongs=H4599&t=KJV.

Chapter 5: Zion Heart

1. *Merriam-Webster*, s.v. "shine," accessed September 20, 2019, https://www.merriam-webster.com/dictionary/shine.

2. Blue Letter Bible, s.v. "*nataph*," accessed September 20, 2019, https://www.blueletterbible.org/lang/lexicon/lexicon.cfm?Strongs=H5197&t=KJV.

3. "What Is a Prophet/Prophetess?" TruthorTradition.com, accessed September 20, 2019, https://www.truthortradition.com/articles/what-is-a-prophet-prophetess.

4. Robert I. Holmes, *In the Footsteps of Elisha* (n.p.: Storm Harvest, 2006), 62, https://docplayer.net/55317174-In-the-footsteps-of-elisha-by-robert-i-holmes-discovering-the-prophetic-gift-in-all-its-fullness.html.

5.   *Merriam-Webster,* s.v. "distill," accessed September 21, 2019, https://www.merriam-webster.com/dictionary/distill.

6.   "Hebrew Words for Prophets and Seers," TruthfortheLastDays .com, accessed September 21, 2019, http://www.truthforthelastdays.com /baptismandgifts/baptismandgifts36.html.

7.   Dictionary.com, s.v. "guile," accessed September 21, 2019, https://www.dictionary.com/browse/guile?s=t.

8.   Bible Hub, s.v. "Isaiah 56:3," Barnes' Notes on the Bible, accessed September 22, 2019, https://biblehub.com/nasb/isaiah/56-3.htm.

9.   Blue Letter Bible, s.v. *"shalem,"* accessed September 22, 2019, https://www.blueletterbible.org/lang/lexicon/lexicon .cfm?Strongs=H8003&t=KJV.

CHAPTER 6: WORSHIP—THE DOORWAY TO THE GLORY REALM

1.   *Merriam-Webster,* s.v. "prophet," accessed September 26, 2019, https://www.merriam-webster.com/dictionary/prophet.

2.   *Cambridge Dictionary,* s.v. "prophesy," accessed September 26, 2019, https://dictionary.cambridge.org/dictionary/english/prophesy.

3.   Blue Letter Bible, s.v. *"halal,"* accessed September 25, 2019, https://www.blueletterbible.org/lang/lexicon/lexicon .cfm?Strongs=H1984&t=KJV.

4.   Blue Letter Bible, s.v. *"yadah,"* accessed September 25, 2019, https://www.blueletterbible.org/lang/lexicon/lexicon .cfm?Strongs=H3034&t=KJV.

5.   Blue Letter Bible, s.v. *"towdah,"* accessed September 25, 2019, https://www.blueletterbible.org/lang/lexicon/lexicon .cfm?Strongs=H8426&t=KJV.

6.   Blue Letter Bible, s.v. *"shabach,"* accessed September 25, 2019, https://www.blueletterbible.org/lang/lexicon/lexicon .cfm?Strongs=H7623&t=KJV.

7.   Blue Letter Bible, s.v. *"barak,"* accessed September 25, 2019, https://www.blueletterbible.org/lang/lexicon/lexicon .cfm?Strongs=H1288&t=KJV.

8.   Blue Letter Bible, s.v. *"zamar,"* accessed September 23, 2019, https://www.blueletterbible.org/lang/lexicon/lexicon .cfm?Strongs=H2167&t=KJV.

9.   "Hebrew Words for Praise," accessed September 25, 2019, http://buddysheets.tripod.com/hebrewwordsforpraise.htm.

10.   Lexico Dictionary, s.v. "laud," accessed September 25, 2019, https://www.lexico.com/en/definition/laud.

11.   Blue Letter Bible, s.v. *"zamar,"* accessed September 23, 2019, https://www.blueletterbible.org/lang/lexicon/lexicon .cfm?Strongs=H2167&t=KJV.

CHAPTER 7: THE BLESSINGS OF THE GLORY (PART 1)—THE GLORY REALM

1.   Dictionary.com, s.v. "realm," accessed September 23, 2019, https://www.dictionary.com/browse/realm.

2.   Bible Study Tools, s.v. *"kabowd,"* accessed September 23, 2019, https://www.biblestudytools.com/lexicons/hebrew/nas/kabowd.html.

3.   Bible Study Tools, s.v. *"doxa,"* accessed September 25, 2019, https://www.biblestudytools.com/lexicons/greek/kjv/doxa.html.

4.   Bible Hub, s.v. "5278. *noam,"* accessed September 25, 2019, https://biblehub.com/hebrew/5278.htm.

5.   Bible Hub, s.v. "1347. *ga'own,"* accessed September 25, 2019, https://biblehub.com/hebrew/1347.htm.

6.   Thesaurus.com, s.v. "glory," accessed September 25, 2019, https://www.thesaurus.com/browse/glory?s=t

7.   *Merriam-Webster* (thesaurus), s.v. "majesty," accessed September 23, 2019, https://www.merriam-webster.com/dictionary/majesty.

8.   *Merriam-Webster* (thesaurus), s.v. "arise," accessed September 23, 2019, https://www.merriam-webster.com/thesaurus/arise.

9.   *Merriam-Webster,* s.v. "shine," accessed September 23, 2019, https://www.merriam-webster.com/thesaurus/shine.

10.   Glenn Pease, "The Jewels of Heaven," Faith Life Sermons, accessed September 23, 2019, https://sermons.faithlife.com /sermons/124750-the-jewels-of-heaven.

11.   Bible Hub, s.v. "5247. huperoché," accessed September 25, 2019, https://biblehub.com/greek/5247.htm.

12.   "El Shaddai—the Breasted One, or Who's That Lady," GoodNewsInc.net, accessed September 25, 2019, http://goodnewsinc.net /wisdom/shaddai.html.

13.   Bible Hub, s.v. "7965. shalom," accessed September 25, 2019, https://biblehub.com/hebrew/7965.htm.

14.   "Solomon," Behind the Name, accessed September 23, 2019, https://www.behindthename.com/name/solomon.

15.   Bible Tools, s.v. *"sozo,"* accessed September 25, 2019, https://www. bibletools.org/index.cfm/fuseaction/Lexicon.show/ID/G4982/sozo.htm.

16.   Lexico Dictionary, s.v. "salvation," accessed September 26, 2019, https://www.lexico.com/en/definition/salvation.

CHAPTER 8: THE BLESSINGS OF THE GLORY (PART 2)—YOU CAN'T STAY SMALL

1.   Brian Houston (@BrianCHouston), "Smallness inside a man (smallness of thinking and spirit) will shrink his world, shrink his children, and shrink his potential," Twitter, December 30, 2017, 5:27 p.m., https://twitter.com/BrianCHouston/status/947277906979332096.

2.   *Merriam-Webster*, s.v. "arise," accessed September 28, 2019, https://www.merriam-webster.com/dictionary/arise.

3.   Blue Letter Bible, s.v. *"chayil,"* accessed September 25, 2019, https://www.blueletterbible.org/lang/lexicon/lexicon .cfm?Strongs=H2428&t=KJV.

4.   Blue Letter Bible, s.v. *"lebab,"* accessed September 25, 2019, https://www.blueletterbible.org/lang/lexicon/lexicon .cfm?Strongs=H3824&t=KJV.

5.   Bible Hub, s.v. "jasper," accessed September 23, 2019, https://biblehub.com/topical/j/jasper.htm.

6.   Bible Hub, s.v. "jasper."

7.   *Cambridge Dictionary*, s.v. "upgrade," accessed September 25, 2019, https://dictionary.cambridge.org/us/dictionary/english/upgrade.

8.   Bible Study Tools, s.v. "Revelation 21:16," accessed September 24, 2019, https://www.biblestudytools.com/commentaries/revelation /revelation-21/revelation-21-16.html.

9.   Bible Study Tools, s.v. *"Megas,"* accessed September 24, 2019, https://www.biblestudytools.com/lexicons/greek/nas/megas.html.

CHAPTER 9: THE WEIGHT OF GLORY

1.   Bible Study Tools, s.v. *"kabowd,"* accessed September 24, 2019, https://www.biblestudytools.com/lexicons/hebrew/nas/kabowd.html.

2.   Study Light, s.v. "glory," accessed September 24, 2019, https://www.studylight.org/dictionaries/hbd/g/glory.html.

3.   albinomexican, "The Heaviness of God," *Lens Crafting* (blog), April 1, 2009, https://joshmcclellan.wordpress.com/2009/04/01 /the-heaviness-of-god/.

4.   Jennifer Eivaz, "When the weighty glory (Hebrew: kabod) comes upon you, think of it as the 'heavyweight' anointing," Facebook, July 15, 2017, https://www.facebook.com/jennifereivaz/posts/when-the -weighty-glory-hebrew-kabod-comes-upon-you-think-of-it-as-the-heavy -weig/1005293069613617/. The word *kavod* means weight or heaviness. Thus to experience the glory of God is to feel the weight of God. To know God's glory is for Him to be heavy upon us. It is a rich concept with a number of implications.

5. Mary Fairchild, "How Heavy Was a Talent in the Bible?" Learn Religions, accessed September 24, 2019, https://www.learnreligions.com/what-is-a-talent-700699.

6. Urban Dictionary, s.v. "heavyweight," accessed September 24, 2019, https://www.urbandictionary.com/define.php?term=heavyweight.

CHAPTER 10: THE AUTHORITY AND STRENGTH OF THE ZION BELIEVER

1. Blue Letter Bible, s.v. "mashal," accessed September 25, 2019, https://www.blueletterbible.org/lang/lexicon/lexicon.cfm?Strongs=H4910&t=KJV.

2. Julian Sinclair, "Eshet Chayil," TheJC.com, November 5, 2008, https://www.thejc.com/judaism/jewish-words/eshet-chayil-1.5966.

3. Bible Hub, s.v. "381. ish-chayil," accessed September 25, 2019, https://biblehub.com/hebrew/381.htm.

4. Tim Brown, "Gibbor-Chayil: Are You One?" REUP: Men Living by Life, April 2015, https://myemail.constantcontact.com/GIBBOR-CHAYIL---Are-you-one-.html?soid=1111234994442&aid=QyI9gfu2Khw.

5. Blue Letter Bible, s.v. "chayil."

6. "What Is Chayil?" Chayil Women International, accessed September 25, 2019, https://chayilwomenintl.org/index.php/chayil-learning-centre/frequently-asked-questions.

7. Blue Letter Bible, s.v. "chayil."

8. Blue Letter Bible, s.v. "chayil."

9. Oxford Living Dictionaries, s.v. "efficient," accessed September 25, 2019, https://en.oxforddictionaries.com/definition/efficient; Oxford Living Dictionaries (thesaurus), s.v. "efficient," accessed September 25, 2019, https://en.oxforddictionaries.com/thesaurus/efficient.

10. Blue Letter Bible, s.v. "gĕbuwrah," accessed September 25, 2019, https://www.blueletterbible.org/lang/lexicon/lexicon.cfm?Strongs=H1369&t=KJV.

11. Bible Study Tools, s.v. "dunamis," accessed September 25, 2019, https://www.biblestudytools.com/lexicons/greek/kjv/dunamis.html.

12. Bible Study Tools, s.v. "dunamis."

13. Blue Letter Bible, s.v. "elohim," accessed September 25, 2019, https://www.blueletterbible.org/lang/lexicon/lexicon.cfm?Strongs=H430&t=KJV.

14. Blue Letter Bible, s.v. "gibborw," accessed September 25, 2019, https://www.blueletterbible.org/lang/lexicon/lexicon.cfm?strongs=H1368.

15. Kurt Selles, "El Gibbor: 'The Mighty God,'" RefrrameMedia.com, accessed September 25, 2019, https://today.reframemedia.com/devotions/el-gibbor-the-mighty-god-2014-05-08.

16. Blue Letter Bible, s.v. "*chayil*," accessed September 25, 2019, https://www.blueletterbible.org/lang/lexicon/lexicon.cfm?strongs=H2428.

17. Lexico Dictionary, s.v. "force," accessed September 25, 2019, https://www.lexico.com/en/definition/force.

18. Lexico (thesaurus), s.v. "force," accessed September 25, 2019, https://www.lexico.com/en/synonym/force.

19. Blue Letter Bible, s.v. "*dynamis*," accessed September 25, 2019, https://www.blueletterbible.org/lang/lexicon/lexicon.cfm?t=mgnt&strongs=g1411.

20. Blue Letter Bible, s.v. "*megaleiotēs*," accessed September 25, 2019, https://www.blueletterbible.org/lang/lexicon/lexicon.cfm?Strongs=G3168&t=KJV.

21. *Merriam-Webster*, s.v. "anoint," accessed September 25, 2019, https://www.merriam-webster.com/dictionary/anoint.

22. Blue Letter Bible, s.v. "*qavah*," accessed September 25, 2019, https://www.blueletterbible.org/lang/lexicon/lexicon.cfm?t=kjv&strongs=h6960.

23. Blue Letter Bible, s.v. "*qavah*."

24. Blue Letter Bible, s.v. "*qavah*."

25. Bible Hub, s.v. "4752. *strateia*," accessed September 25, 2019, https://biblehub.com/greek/4752.htm.

26. Bible Hub, s.v. "3794. *ochuróma*," accessed September 25, 2019, https://biblehub.com/greek/3794.htm.

27. Bible Hub, s.v. "*logismos*," accessed September 25, 2019, https://biblehub.com/greek/3053.htm.

28. Bible Hub, s.v. "*logismos*."

29. Bible Study Tools, s.v. "*exousia*," accessed September 25, 2019, https://www.biblestudytools.com/lexicons/greek/kjv/exousia.html.

30. Lexico Dictionary, s.v. "authority," accessed September 25, 2019, https://www.lexico.com/en/definition/authority.

31. Bible Hub, s.v. "1369. *geburah*," accessed September 25, 2019, https://biblehub.com/hebrew/1369.htm.

32. Blue Letter Bible, s.v. "*etsah*," accessed September 25, 2019, https://www.blueletterbible.org/lang/lexicon/lexicon.cfm?t=kjv&strongs=h6098.

33. Warren W. Wiersbe, *Bible Expository Commentary: Old Testament Wisdom and Poetry* (Grand Rapids, MI: David C. Cook, 2004), 1:339.

Chapter 11: God's Mercy toward Zion

1.   Blue Letter Bible, s.v. *"checed,"* accessed April 10, 2019, https://www.blueletterbible.org/lang/Lexicon/lexicon.cfm?ot=NASB&strongs=H2617&t=KJV&bn=14.

2.   Lexico Dictionary, s.v. "kindness," accessed September 25, 2019, https://www.lexico.com/en/definition/kindness.

3.   Lexico (thesaurus), s.v. "kindness," accessed September 25, 2019, https://www.lexico.com/en/synonym/kindness.

4.   Iain Duguid, "Loyal-Love (Hesed)," Ligoner.org, accessed September 25, 2019, https://www.ligonier.org/learn/articles/loyal-love-hesed/.

5.   Bible Study Tools, s.v. "mercy seat," accessed September 26, 2019, https://www.biblestudytools.com/encyclopedias/isbe/mercy-seat-the.html.

6.   Lexico (thesaurus), s.v. "magnify," accessed September 25, 2019, https://www.lexico.com/en/synonym/magnify.

7.   Dictionary.com, s.v. "magnify," accessed September 25, 2019, https://www.dictionary.com/browse/magnify?s=t.

8.   "What Is the Middle Verse of the Bible?" House to House, accessed September 25, 2019, https://housetohouse.com/middle-verse-bible/.

9.   Lexico Dictionary, s.v. "comfort," accessed September 26, 2019, https://www.lexico.com/en/definition/comfort.